Dedicated to all the Red Sneaker Writers:
You can't fail unless you quit.

Perfecting Plot

Charting the Hero's Journey

Perfecting Plot: Charting the Hero's Journey

First Edition

Copyright © 2013 William Bernhardt Writing Programs

Red Sneaker Press

An imprint of Babylon Books

ISBN: 978-0-9893789-2-5

Perfecting Plot
Charting the Hero's Journey

William Bernhardt

The Red Sneaker Writer Series

Other Books by William Bernhardt

Red Sneaker Writer Series

Story Structure: The Key to Successful Fiction
Creating Character: Bringing Your Story to Life
Perfecting Plot: Charting the Hero's Journey
The Fundamentals of Fiction (DVD)

The Ben Kincaid Series

Primary Justice
Blind Justice
Deadly Justice
Perfect Justice
Cruel Justice
Naked Justice
Extreme Justice
Dark Justice
Silent Justice

Murder One
Criminal Intent
Hate Crime
Death Row
Capitol Murder
Capitol Threat
Capitol Conspiracy
Capitol Offense
Capitol Betrayal

Other Novels

The Code of Buddyhood
Paladins of the Abyss
Dark Eye
The Midnight Before
Christmas
Final Round

Nemesis: The Final Case of
Eliot Ness
Double Jeopardy
Strip Search
The Idea Man
Shine

Poetry

The White Bird

For Young Readers

Equal Justice: The Courage of Ada Lois Sipuel (biography)
Princess Alice and the Dreadful Dragon (illus. by Kerry McGhee)
The Black Sentry

Edited by William Bernhardt

Legal Briefs
Natural Suspect

Plot: Stuff happens to people you care about.

John D McDonald

TABLE OF CONTENTS

INTRODUCTION

Welcome to the third book in the Red Sneaker Writers series. If you've read other Red Sneaker publications or attended Red Sneaker events, you can skip to Chapter One. If you're new, let me take a moment to explain.

I've been writing for many years, doing almost every kind of writing imaginable. I've been speaking at writing workshops and conferences almost as long. Every time I step behind the podium I see the same tableau staring back at me: long rows of talented people, most of whom have attended many conferences, frustrated by the fact that they haven't sold a book. And wondering why. Yes, the market is tough and agents are hard to find yadda yadda yadda whine whine whine excuse excuse excuse. But when aspiring writers do the work, put it out there, but still don't publish…there's usually a reason. Too often enormous potential is lost due to a lack of fundamental knowledge. Sometimes a little guidance is all that stands between an unpublished writer and a satisfying writing career.

I do my best to help at conferences, but the large auditorium/general information lecture is not terribly conducive to writing instruction. And sometimes what I've heard other instructors say was not particularly helpful. Too often people seemed more interested in appearing "literary" than in providing useful information. Sometimes I felt that speakers did more to obfuscate the subject than explain it, that they wanted to make writing as mysterious and incomprehensible as possible, either because that made them sound more erudite or because they didn't understand the subject themselves. How is that going to help anyone get published?

After giving this problem some thought, I formulated the Red Sneaker Writing Center. Why Red Sneakers? Because I love my red sneakers. They're practical, flexible, sturdy—and bursting with style and flair. In other words, exactly what I think writing instruction should be. Practical, flexible, useful, but still designed to unleash the creative spirit, to give the imagination a platform for creating wondrous work.

I held the first Red Sneaker Writers conference in 2005. I invited the best teachers I knew, not only people who had published many books but people who could teach. Then I launched my small-group seminars—five intensive days of work with seven or so aspiring writers. This gave me the opportunity to read, edit, and work one-on-one with individuals, so I could target their needs and make sure they got what would help them most. This approach worked extremely well and I'm proud to say a substantial list of writers have graduated from my seminars and published work with major publishers. But not everyone is able to attend my seminars. How could I help them?

This book, and the other books in this series, are designed to provide assistance to writers regardless of their location. The books are short, inexpensive, and targeted to specific areas where a writer might want assistance.

Let me see if I can anticipate your questions:

Why are these books so short? Because I've expunged the unnecessary and the unhelpful. I've pared it down to the essential information, practical and useful ideas that can improve your writing. Too many instructional books are padded to fill word counts required by book contracts. That's not the Red Sneaker way.

Why are you writing so many different books instead of one big book? I encourage writers to commit to writing every day (see Appendix F) and to maintain a consistent writing schedule (see Appendix E). You can read these books without losing much writing time. In fact, each can be read in a single afternoon. Take one day off from your writing schedule. Read and make notes in the margins. See if that doesn't trigger ideas for your own work.

I bet it will. And the next day, you can get back to your writing.

You reference other books as examples, but you rarely quote excerpts from them. Why?

Two reasons. First, I'm trying to keep the books brief. If you want to look up a passage from a book, it's easy enough to do. Second, if I quote from materials currently under copyright protection, I have to pay a fee to the copyright owner, which means I'd need to raise the price of this book to cover the fee. I don't want to do that. I think you can grasp my points without reading copyrighted excerpts. Too often, in my opinion, excessive excerpting in writing books is done to pad the page count.

Why does each chapter end with exercises?

The exercises are a completely integrated and essential part of this book. Samuel Johnson was correct when he wrote: *Scribendo disces scribere.* Meaning: You learn to write by writing. I can gab on and on, but these principles won't be concretized in your brain until you put them into practice. So don't get in such a hurry that you don't get the full benefit from this book. Take the time to complete the exercises, because they may improve your next writing effort. If you were in one of my small-group seminars, this would be your homework. I won't be hovering over your shoulder when you read this book—but you should do the exercises anyway.

What else does the Red Sneaker Writers Center do?

I send out a free monthly newsletter filled with writing advice, market analysis, and other items of interest. If you'd like to be added to the mailing list, visit: http://www.williambernhardt.com/writing_instruction/index.php. There are three books in this series so far and there will be more in the future. We hold an annual writing conference with a very specific focus: getting you the information you need to publish. I lead small-group seminars every summer. The newsletter will provide dates and information about these programs.

You may also be interested in my DVD set, *The Fundamentals of Fiction*, available at Amazon or on my website. It's about five hours of me talking about writing. Who doesn't want that?

Okay, enough of this warm-up act. Read this. Then write your book. Follow your dreams. Never give up.

William Bernhardt

CHAPTER 1: UNDERSTANDING PLOT

Writing fiction is the act of weaving a series of lies to arrive at a greater truth.

Khaled Hosseini

Y ou may not think plot is all that difficult to understand, or to put it a different way, you may not think there's all that much to understand about plot. It's just making up stuff up. Figuring out what happens next, right?

Wrong. There's much more to it, and until you understand that, you're unlikely to come up with the plot that best serves your characters and snares readers into an unforgettable reading experience. If you've read my book, *Story Structure*, you know the essential elements that must be laid out: the inciting incident, plot points, turning points, climax, and so forth. But knowing what you need is not the same as knowing how to write it. If you've read my book, *Creating Character*, you may know what kind of journey your protagonist needs to take. But knowing where they're going is not the same as knowing how to get them there.

In this book, I'll discuss how you can map out that journey in the most gripping, engaging, exciting way possible, to create a book filled with power and emotion and urgent human need.

So what is plot?

Plot is the writer's choice of events to tell the story of the characters' progression toward their goals or desires.

What Do Your Characters Really Want?

This may be a classic case of a definition that, while accurate, makes this sound more complicated than it has to be. Plot is about the relationship between the characters and the story's structure. Your main characters want something—that's what motivates the action of the book. The protagonist's journey is the movement toward that goal. So when plotting, you decide what steps must be taken to create the journey from where your main character is at the start of the book to where she will be at the end.

There are many possible journeys. Your job as a writer is to determine which is best.

Your protagonist must want something. And there must be something preventing her from immediately obtaining it. That's conflict, the lifeblood of story. This opposition may be represented by an antagonist or antagonists. But there must be some kind of conflict, something that stands in the protagonist's way. Plot will describe the manner by which the conflict leads to action and the action keeps the story moving until it reaches its climax.

A character is defined by the choices he makes under pressure. So for character to be revealed, there must be pressure—which is generated by conflict. When plotting, you must provide enough stressful situations to reveal the character's inner nature.

2

PERFECTING PLOT

You may notice that I can barely say a word about plot without also mentioning character. For good reason. They are two sides of the same coin, working hand in hand to bring your story to life. To quote F. Scott Fitzgerald, "Character is plot; plot is character."

Perhaps you're contemplating a popular fiction blockbuster, so you're thinking you can get by with superficial characters and stereotypes. Bad idea. I can't say it's never been done, but it's the wrong approach, especially if you're hoping to write something wonderful, something that lingers beyond next week's sales reports. Or perhaps you're writing women's fiction, or something literary, so you think plot will not be that important. Maybe you're thinking you can skip this book altogether.

Let's not do anything drastic. Granted, not all books are the same—and that's a good thing. Different books provide different kinds of appeal for different audiences. There are differences between, say, *The Taming of the Shrew* and *The Hunger Games*. But the differences aren't about character, because both have fascinating characters. And the differences aren't about plot either, because both tell engaging stories. So what is the difference?

Let's consider the plots of some recent literary critically acclaimed novels. *Room*, by Emma Donoghue, is about an abducted woman locked in a room and sexually abused for years. This could easily be the plot of a crime novel, and in fact, has been on several prior occasions.

Cormac McCarthy's *The Road* involves a father and son traveling in search of a safe haven in a hideous post-apocalyptic America. This could easily be the plot of a science fiction novel, and in fact, has been on several prior occasions.

Karen Thompson Walker's novel *The Age of Miracles* also tells an end-of-the-world story. How can we say plot doesn't matter in literary fiction when so many tell such high-concept, extraordinary stories?

If you want to write a successful novel, something in the same league with these kinds of books, you must have both memorable plot and memorable characters. You must have vivid, compelling characters and a story replete with urgency and emotional need. The best novels hook you on the first page and don't let you go until the story is over. When you hear someone say, "I couldn't put it down"—that doesn't mean the author is a hack who only cares about plot. That means the writer took great care to perfect and streamline his language so it would convey the essential information about both character and plot without slowing the pace of the story.

Here's the bottom line: **You need both a strong plot and strong characters. The plot must be right for the character, and the character must be right for the plot.**

Matching Characters and Plot

Too often, beginning writers will devise their characters and plots in a vacuum, or to be more specific, in two separate vacuums. They choose a character they find appealing, perhaps a glamourized version of themselves or a mildly altered variation of their favorite character from fiction or the movies. The plot is borne of some idea that came to them somewhere—a dream, a stray thought while showering, a personal experience that still troubles them. The problem is that these two essential elements arose independently from two separate impulses, then were forced upon one another in a mash-up that may or may not work.

They should have arisen from the same impulse. They should have been chosen in conjunction with one another as two closely related elements designed to achieve one goal. Your goal. The reason you're writing this book in the first place. Using a story to say what it is you want to say.

Highlights

1) Regardless of what kind of story you're writing, memorable characters and memorable plot are essential.

2) All stories are character-driven.

3) Character and plot are two closely interrelated ways of viewing the same thing: your story.

4) The plot must be right for the character, and the character must be right for the plot.

Red Sneaker Exercises

1) If you haven't started writing your book, or even if you have, make a writing schedule. Commit to writing a certain number of hours per day (as many as possible) and a certain number of days a week (preferably seven). Now treat that commitment as you would any other job. Show up on time and do what you promised to do. At the end of this book, in Appendix E, you'll find a suggested Writing Schedule. See if you can make it your own. Then check out the Writers Contract attached as Appendix F. Print it out. If you sign it, it will be legally binding, because it was drafted by an actual attorney. Me.

2) Think about the lead character in your book. What makes that character interesting, intriguing, or unique? Now consider what plot might be perfect for that character, either because it allows her to employ her unique

gifts or specialties, or because it will force her to confront her worst fears.

WILLIAM BERNHARDT

CHAPTER 2: PAIRING PLOT AND CHARACTER

What is character but the determination of incident? And what is incident but the illumination of character?

Henry James

Although plot and character are different concepts, and they can be considered independently, they are much better when they go together. In other words, they're not oil and water. They're dinner and a movie. And although you might be able to conjure up one without the other, the savvy writer will consider one as a reflection of the other, the missing jigsaw piece needed to attain the best possible result.

Percolating Plot

Often, I think creative writing instructors overcomplicate matters, but this is an instance where the point cannot be emphasized enough. Character and plot have a symbiotic relationship, and finding the correct match may be the key that transforms your book from ordinary to extraordinary.

Let's consider *The Da Vinci Code*. Since over eighty-one million copies of that novel have been sold, statistically speaking, a few of you might have read it. You remember what the book was about, right?

But do you remember the lead character? Can you think of his name? What's his job? Specifically?

And if you can't remember, why not?

The lead character in that and four other Dan Brown novels is Robert Langdon. He's a Harvard professor of symbology.

No, not symbiology—symbology, which Microsoft Word does not even recognize as a word.

Now that's different. Usually the heroes in thrillers are men of action, tough guys, gunslingers, hard-boiled detectives and the like. In most of those books, Langdon would be worse than useless.

And yet, the hero of the most successful thriller in the history of the world is a professor in a field so arcane most people could not even tell you what it is.

Symbology is the study of symbols, which in this book is the best skill a hero could possibly have because this plot is all about interesting signs and symbols, recognizing the significance of icons in ancient works of art, and solving codes devised hundreds of years ago.

In other words, the character was perfect for the plot, and the plot was perfect for the character.

Sometimes I've suggested that students tweak a character or give him a special ability to make it fit the plot better, only to be met with the response, "That's not realistic."

Is realism what people read novels for? No. A novel must have verisimilitude, that is, the appearance of reality, within the context of the world created by the book. But realism? Here's some realism for you:

PERFECTING PLOT

Harvard doesn't even *have* a department of symbology.

But that completely fictional occupation made for a rip-snorting adventure, just the same. (A passage in the later novel, *Inferno*, suggests that symbology may be a subdivision of Harvard's Art History department. Someone must've tipped Brown off to the problem.)

In my novel, *Dark Eye*, the principal characters are Susan Pulaski, the troubled police psychologist, and Darcy O'Bannon, a young autistic savant. This is a crime novel involving the pursuit of a deranged serial killer taking his inspiration from the works of Edgar Allan Poe (published years before the television series *The Following*). This murderer is brutal, violent, and smart. How will these two unlikely partners catch him?

Let's think a moment about the two entities I chose to lead this story. A brainiac psych (suffering serious emotional problems) and a young man with a neurological dysfunction who has never worked a day in his life. Seems unlikely, doesn't it? Truth is, in most crime novels, they couldn't crack the case. They probably couldn't solve a jaywalking.

But for the case in *Dark Eye*, they're perfect. Because this case involves a madman suffering from an extreme case of aberrant behavior. Taking his inspiration from the works of Poe, particularly an obscure work of cosmology titled *Eureka*, "Edgar" recreates scenes from Poe's work. Because Poe was fascinated with cryptograms (and quite good at them), "Edgar" leaves a series of messages in a triple-encrypted code that even computers are unable to solve.

To the Las Vegas police department, this case looks hopeless. Unless they can find: 1) someone with true insight into extreme aberrant behavior, 2) someone with a keen gift for noticing the unusual, 3) someone who knows Poe's work inside-out, and 4) someone with a savant gift for puzzle-solving.

In other words, Susan and Darcy. Susan has the psychological profiling background needed understand the twisted mind of the killer. But she's not a detective by training. Unlike Sherlock Holmes, she's not going to look at the dirt on someone's sneakers and say, "Oh, I see you've been to Afghanistan."

But Darcy might. As a result of his neurodiversity, he notices the unusual, what other people miss. Furthermore, because he has an eidetic memory, and his father has an extensive library of classics, he knows the work of Poe so well that he can tell what page of the book a certain passage appeared upon. Furthermore, he has the savant ability to solve puzzles essentially just by looking at them, without even being able to explain how he reached his solution. So yes, in another case, these two might not be particularly helpful. But in this case...

The plot is perfect for the characters, and the characters are perfect for the plot.

That does not happen by accident. That comes as a result of careful and strategic planning. In the sequel, *Strip Search*, Susan and Darcy confront another very different killer, but one that once again allows Susan to exercise her psychological insight. Moreover, because the killer is a mathematician obsessed with numbers, Darcy's autistic gifts once again prove invaluable. Character matches plot; plot matches character.

PERFECTING PLOT

Special Abilities

Often I encourage writers to give their lead character special powers or abilities, and perhaps now you can see why. By giving your character that uniqueness, you explain why you've chosen that person to be the viewpoint character, or to put it a different way, why we're watching this story unfold through that character's eyes.

More than one critic complained that my character, the lawyer Ben Kincaid, is the wrong man to lead a series of thrillers, because he's so timid and reserved and unassuming and physically clumsy and...well, unlike all the other thriller heroes. What they missed was—that's the whole point. That's what makes him stand out from the crowd. Some readers may not care for him, but those who do like him a whole lot, because he's different and flawed and thus easier for them to embrace.

Those critics also missed Ben's special abilities, the ones often taken for granted in fiction but that are critical in the Ben Kincaid novels.

For instance: Ben is smart. Not just a little smart. Very very smart. And he's tenacious. When he has a thousand reasons to give up a case and move on to something more lucrative, he doesn't. Even when the odds are stacked hopelessly against him, he never stops trying.

Most importantly—and I believe this is the true enduring appeal of the character—he genuinely cares about his clients. It shows. He doesn't have to say it. You can tell. And that's what readers want more than anything else. In an age that can be quite cynical about lawyers, here's one who really cares. A lawyer who isn't in it just to plump up his bank account or put a swimming pool in his backyard.

A lawyer who genuinely sympathizes with others and wants to help them if he can.

In other words, although Ben is no superhero, he does have special abilities that single him out from other characters and make him uniquely qualified to handle certain cases.

Did Ben's personality affect the kinds of cases he tackled? Of course. In *Cruel Justice*, he represents a developmentally disabled youth, shuttled through the legal system for a decade, because the boy's father appeals to Ben's innate sense of justice. In *Perfect Justice*, Ben represents a white supremacist he finds completely odious, because he realizes that if he doesn't, the man will not receive a fair trial, and he strongly believes that all defendants have a constitutional right to a fair trial. In *Silent Justice*, the corporation opposing his client literally tries to bankrupt Ben, assuming that a lawyer's heart is in his wallet. But Ben never backs down.

Ben Kincaid's special qualities, which may not be immediately apparent to some readers, make him uniquely qualified to handle the plots I conceived for him.

So as you construct your plot, think about what makes your character different. What makes her more interesting than the average person? And what special gifts might your characters bring to the obstacles they'll confront throughout the story. If you're writing a science fiction novel, they may literally have superpowers. If you're writing a quieter literary novel, it may be an inner resilience or fortitude. It can be many different qualities—but make sure there's something. Give your readers a reason to spend time with this individual.

Those who have read my book on character will recall the discussion of character arc. What journey is your character on? What is her quest, her goal, her heart's desire? I raise this because it will also influence your decision regarding plot. You must construct a plot that challenges the character and leads them on the journey you want them to have. You must create a conflict that convincingly describes the character's development from where they are at the beginning of the book to where you want them to be when they reach the climax.

Comfort Zone

Don't be misled by the preceding discussion into thinking this means you must always create plots that show your characters at their finest. Sometimes exactly the opposite can be more exciting. You're still matching character to plot—just in a perverse way. Torturing your characters instead of showing them in their best light. And that's what being a writer is all about. Torturing your characters for fun and profit.

For instance, as I've mentioned Ben has deep social anxieties, inhibitions, and insecurities. So was it a coincidence that, in one of my favorite entries in the series, *Extreme Justice*, Ben is forced to continue his investigation—in a nudist camp? Did I do that so I could show him at his best? Hardly. I did it so I should show him refusing to give up, persevering, despite his extreme discomfort (and perhaps so readers could have a little fun along the way). Why, in the first book in the series, *Primary Justice*, did I send this poor innocent naïf into a strip club? Same reason. By the time of *Capitol Murder*, Ben is forced to enter Washington inner circles, and he's not even particularly interested in politics. The other characters keep assuming he's a Democrat because he's a defense attorney and frequently represents the little guy. Ben doesn't know what they're talking about. He's just wants to help out a childhood friend. But his determination causes him to plunge ahead into many circles he would prefer to avoid.

Don't be afraid to take your characters out of their comfort zones. This means, first, that you must know what those comfort zones are. Understand who your characters are, then see if you can write a story that forces them to do something they would never do by choice. Unfortunately, they're in the hands of a devilish writer determined to plunge them into extraordinary circumstances—because that's makes for interesting plotting.

Series Characters

Series characters present a special difficulty for those attempting to formulate the perfect match between character and plot. I'm not talking about multi-part epics that basically tell one large story (i.e., *The Lord of the Rings*). I'm referring to series characters who recur in separate, self-contained stories (James Bond, Cotton Malone, Dirk Pitt).

Typically, in the first entry in a good series, the writer will match character and plot effectively. That's what makes the plot tick and the character work. But then what? Just as the authors of series characters often have difficulty repeatedly devising character journeys for the protagonist, so they can also be stymied by the problem of repeatedly matching character and plot. The character already has been established. How do you come up with a different plot that works?

Characters, like real people, are complex and multifaceted. They cannot be defined by a single trait or ability. Consequently, different stories can exploit different talents they may have in their tool belt, or explore different aspects of their personality.

The bad answer is that the author keeps exploiting the same talent or quality over and over again, until eventually the series grows stale and readers stop reading.

Guess which I think is better?

Remember that you can never let your series character become the "host" of someone else's story. If the series character is not the central character, if the story is not organic to him—you've got problems. After awhile, such adventures will stop seeming like novels and start seeming like episodes in a television series where nothing ever changes because producers fear viewers may miss an episode or watch them out of order.

You can do better—if you know your character well. You're a complex character, right? Think of all the trouble you've managed to get into in your life. Now see if you can't do the same for your series characters. A series can continue for a long time and become a staple in your writing career (if that's what you want). But only if you work hard to keep it fresh, keep the plots diverse and interesting, and make sure the plot is always perfectly matched to the character.

Highlights

1) Your plot must be right for your character, and your character must be right for your plot.

2) Special abilities or qualities can make protagonists more interesting—and more capable of dealing with the obstacles in your plot.

3) Never be afraid to take your characters out of their comfort zone.

4) To prevent series characters from becoming stale, allow them to evolve or develop new abilities and talents they either didn't have or the reader didn't know about in previous entries.

5) The main character is always the protagonist, even if this is a series character who has appeared in many previous books. Don't allow them to become a guest star in their own book.

Red Sneaker Exercises

1) Think about who your characters are. If you have my book *Creating Character*, complete the Character Detail Sheet for both your protagonist and your antagonist. Take your time. Do you know as much about these critical characters as you should? What are their special powers or abilities?

2) Now that you've identified your protagonist's special abilities, what plot would show those abilities to their best advantage?

3) What plot development will take your characters out of their comfort zones? How can you show the characters engaging in activities they personally dislike to advance their quest?

4) Are you considering the possibility of making your protagonist a series character? If so, how will you keep the series fresh?

WILLIAM BERNHARDT

CHAPTER 3: PLOT IS CONFLICT

The king died and then the queen died is a story.
The king died, and then the queen died of grief is a plot.

E. M. Forster

I started this chapter with that wonderful quote from Forster's collection of Cambridge lectures, *Aspects of the Novel*, because it so beautifully illustrates the difference between telling a story and constructing a plot. If you've ever heard a small child tell a story, it's a long series of "And then this happened. And then this happened. And then this happened…" That's a story, sure.

But a plot asks an additional question: Why?

Story alone might keep readers attentive for a short time, but eventually they're going to want to know more about the people involved. In other words, they're going to want to know the answer to Forster's question. Why? That's what your plot is designed to explain—while also enthralling the reader on every single page.

Were you shocked in the last chapter when I said you should torture your characters? Most writers are kindly gentle sorts who in real life wouldn't hurt the guy who stole their parking space, much less torture anyone. But if you're planning to write fiction, that's an essential element of your job description, so you're just going to have to get over it.

Conflict is essential to story. What sound is to music, conflict is to story. Without conflict, there is no story. This doesn't mean characters have to be bickering all the time. There are many forms of conflict. Your plot is constructed by deciding upon the primary conflicts and then unfolding them to do the maximum possible damage.

Plot is composed of a series of escalating conflicts.

The Conflict Checklist

While there are many forms of conflict, some are undeniably better than others. What works best for you depends upon what kind of book you're writing. Just remember, first and foremost—conflict hurts. Conflict causes your characters pain, grief, anxiety, angst. If it doesn't sting, it won't make for a dramatic book. Petty annoyances do not make for great reading experiences.

Please also bear in mind that, even if you're writing a psychological or literary novel, the more concrete you can make your conflict, the more powerful it will be. Conflicts that are entirely abstract, intellectual, or theoretical may make for fascinating discussions in the faculty lounge, but don't typically lead to riveting fiction. Regardless of what kind of conflict you choose, the most important point is that you make your readers understand that this conflict MATTERS. It must be meaningful. The threat must be immediate. The potential consequences must be large, if not overwhelming.

Here is the essential checklist for any primary conflict (as opposed to a subplot) you're considering for your novel:

1) Does it involve a character the reader cares about?

2) Is it sufficiently complex that the resolution of the conflict is not obvious to the reader?

3) Will you be able to complicate and magnify this conflict as the book progresses?

4) Will you be able to resolve this conflict in an emotionally satisfying manner?

Twisting the Knife

Your story kicks off with the inciting incident, something so horrible or shocking that it sets the protagonist's life into chaos. At that point, the plot begins. It may start relatively small—but it must be significant enough to keep the reader reading.

Don't shy away from making life horrific for your protagonist. Even if you deeply empathize with the character, it's still your job to keep tightening the screws. This isn't something you do just to extract sadist pleasure. You do it because, first, you want the reader to feel for your character, and readers tend to care about those confronting tough challenges. Furthermore, you want the reader to experience a cathartic feeling of pleasure when, despite incredible obstacles, your protagonist overcomes the opposition (usually). This feeling of vicarious triumph is one of the principal reasons people read novels.

The plot should present increasingly difficult challenges resulting in increasingly difficult problems that are not alleviated until the climax.

Generally speaking, there are three ways to make your protagonist's already-bad situation worse: 1) by raising the stakes, 2) by making his already slim chances of success slimmer, and 3) by making it personal (i.e., by putting someone or something close to the protagonist in danger).

But why? Why do I want to do these horrible things to my lovely characters?

Here's why: Sometimes life can be hard. Almost unbearable. One damn thing after the next. To quote *Buffy the Vampire Slayer*: The hardest thing in the world is to live in it. In the world of recovery, there's a cliché that no addict starts to recover until they hit rock bottom. This is complete balderdash, because in reality, there's no rock bottom. There's no end to the amount of badness this universe is capable of throwing at you.

I don't mention this to depress anyone, but to make a point about why you force your characters to suffer. In real life, most people encounter hardship, be it broken relationships, divorce, problems with children or parents, disease, death, or other challenges. Sometimes despair and depression seem overwhelming. Sometimes you fight the temptation to pull the covers over your head and not even get out of bed.

But much comfort can be found between the pages of a book. Much inspiration can be obtained by experiencing the trials of a protagonist who encounters incredible opposition but refuses to let it stop her. When you feel like you're all alone in the world, books tell you that you're not. When you feel like you're the most miserable, most cursed person on the face of the earth, books tell you that others have felt and still feel exactly the same way. You thought you were the only one? You're not.

Books tell us that we're all far more alike than we're different, that we're all united in the community of humanity.

So yes, it may seem cruel to put your character through these terrible paces. But they will experience great inspiration and exhilaration when they overcome these obstacles. And so will your reader. So don't back away from it. The question is never: How can I give this poor slob a break? The question is always: How can I make my hero's situation worse?

Tension

If you intend to keep your readers riveted to the page, you cannot let the suspense diminish. Not for a page. Not even for a sentence. You can allow the occasional release occasioned by a well-timed bit of humor or a small breakthrough. But overall, the situation must remain grim, dire, and desperate.

Some instructors use the term "tension" to describe this process. Tension is sometimes described as "micro-conflict," that is, the feeling that something isn't right even when you don't quite know what it is yet because the conflict hasn't been fully revealed to you. These are good principles, but it may be simpler to just put the conflict in place as soon as possible and not let it sag until the climax is fully and finally resolved. Infuse each and every page with a sense of urgency—something is wrong, there's a conflict to be resolved, and it must be resolved soon or it will be too late.

Every scene must have an event that changes the character's situation—as a result of conflict. No padding. No walks around the park. Include the events that matter, that advance the narrative, that heighten the tension—and leave everything else out. Backstory and character detail should be integrated into a scene where something happens—but never allowed to slow it down. Please also remember that you don't have to provide all those character details the first moment a character walks upon your stage. The withholding of key information can be a great way to create tension. It leaves readers wondering, What's going on here?

That's what keeps them reading.

Failure

Sometimes I think readers are negatively influenced by film and particularly television, in the sense that they think their hero has to succeed at every turn or they're not heroes any more. This is completely wrong

The protagonist should fail many times before succeeding.

For some of you, this will make immediate sense. If you're writing a novel, you don't want it to end in chapter one, so there must be complications. Many complications. The main conflict must become more complex, and you probably need a few knotty subplots as well. This is what propels your story forward. And to maintain reader interest, it's not enough to just keep having bad stuff happen. The obstacles must intensify. There must be a sense that it's getting worse and worse. That's what makes a story dramatic, and that's also when the reader learns who your protagonist truly is and what he's made of.

Forgive me for using films as an example, but I need a reference point almost all readers will recognize. Question: Which movie did you think was better? *The Empire Strikes Back* or *Return of the Jedi.*

I'm betting you didn't even have to think about that. For most people, from one end of the globe to another, the answer is easy: *Empire*. Why? They're both good movies, with mostly the same characters played by the same actors telling essentially the same story. Okay, there were no Ewoks in *Empire*, but that's not the main difference. If you're familiar with the terminology of Structure, you recognize that *Empire* was Act 2 and *Jedi* was Act 3. *Jedi* had the massive advantage of wrapping up all the plot threads. So why do people prefer *Empire*?

Because it's more exciting when things are going badly for your characters than it is when they're going well.

In *Empire*, the rebels get their butts kicked. Lando betrays Leia and the others, Luke is dismembered and almost killed, and Han is encased in carbonite. And that's how the movie ends.

In *Return*, everything gets fixed and the Empire is defeated. Perhaps a little too easily. Seeing everything fall apart was more thrilling.

This may be another perverse reflection of human nature, but when the world is going to hell, our eyes are riveted to the page. When things are all nicey-nice, our attention tends to wander. Every English major knows *Paradise Lost* is a heck of a lot more interesting than *Paradise Regained*.

You want your readers to be riveted to the page. So let the conflict get increasingly worse, right up to the Turning Point that links Act 2 to Act 3, often called the "crisis" or "dark moment." And don't relieve the tension until the climax is over.

Subplots

The book on structure discusses the value of subplots and how they can maintain reader interest while the primary conflict unfolds. But you may be wondering how to construct a good subplot. If there are four rules for creating a great primary conflict, are there similar rules for creating a great subplot?

Yes, there are. And they're exactly the same four rules. Plus one more: Your subplot must relate in some way to the main conflict.

Your subplot must have some bearing on the primary storyline. Look at your outline. If you've got a subplot that could be completely cut without affecting the progress or outcome of the main plot in the slightest—get rid of it. Or revise it so it does bear on the main plot. If it's completely distinct from the main story, readers will see it as a distraction, a sideshow, and they'll resent it rather than enjoy it. They'll start to skim, not read. Subplots should broaden the story, not slow it down.

You probably won't spend as many words developing your subplot as your do your main conflict. You shouldn't, because if you do, it will confuse the reader about which is the dominant plot. But that doesn't mean the subplot isn't important.

Your book will undoubtedly have supporting characters, and the subplot may be where those characters get to shine. Let a subplot revolve around the best friend, the colleague, the love interest. Your book will be stronger if the subject of the subplot is closely connected to your protagonist.

How many subplots can you have? That depends upon the size and scope of your book. But generally speaking, I think two or three is enough, and more is probably asking for trouble. Tough enough to juggle three plotlines and keep them tense, exciting, and intensifying in complexity. Handling more borders on the impossible.

Please also note that, unlike your main conflict, subplots do not have to span the entire length of the book, though they can. Reference the book on structure for a longer discussion of this principle.

Victory

You can occasionally allow your protagonist to experience small victories. She can rescue the busload of children, so long as the bomb that will incinerate the Magic Kingdom is still set to detonate in fifteen minutes. Your heroine can learn the truth about her true love's mysterious past, so long as there are still seemingly impossible obstacles preventing their union. Minor triumphs are acceptable, and may in fact be necessary to prevent your protagonist from seeming completely incompetent. Just make sure that what is left undone vastly exceeds what has been accomplished. Make sure that the unresolved threat exceeds the problem that has been resolved. And make sure it stays that way, right up to the last sentence of the climax.

If you work in the corporate world, you may have heard the expression, "Two steps forward, one step back." Not a bad approach to plotting, except I would make it, "One step forward, five steps back." That's what keeps it interesting.

Highlights

1) Plot is composed of a series of escalating conflicts.

2) Plot should present increasingly difficult challenges resulting in increasingly difficult problems that are not alleviated until the climax ends.

3) The protagonist should fail many times before succeeding.

4) Subplots must relate to, and enhance, the primary conflict.

5) A good conflict will directly involve a sympathetic protagonist, be meaningful, increase in intensity as the book progresses, and lead to an emotionally satisfying resolution.

Red Sneaker Exercises

1) You've probably already formulated in your mind what the basic conflict of your book will be. How will you make it worse? And then worse? And then still worse? Will you raise the stakes? Will you make the protagonist's chances of success slimmer? Will you make the danger more personal? Or perhaps, all three.

2) What small success along the way (probably in the midst of Act 2) can you give your hero, if only to

prevent her from seeming like a complete screw-up? And then, after she's basked in her brief and minor moment of success, how can you make everything get a thousand times worse?

3) Ask yourself the four questions in the "Conflict Checklist" presented earlier in this chapter. Can you answer each of those questions about your main plot and subplots in a satisfying way?

a) Does it involve a character the reader cares about?

b) Is it sufficiently complex that the resolution of the conflict is not obvious to the reader?

c) Will you be able to complicate and magnify this conflict as the book progresses?

d) Will you be able to resolve this conflict in an emotionally satisfying manner?

WILLIAM BERNHARDT

CHAPTER 4: THE FACE OF CONFLICT

He that struggles with us strengthens our nerves and sharpens our skill. Our antagonist is our helper.

Edmund Burke

I n the best stories, the antagonist will have real human motivations rather than clichés or easy excuses for evil. Since we've talked so much about your protagonist, and the necessity that the protagonist face enormous obstacles, it might be useful to consider for a moment the source of that opposition—and how powerful that opposition must be.

The protagonist's story is only as interesting as the antagonist makes it.

Opposition

The typical aspiring writer will spend far more time fleshing out the lead character than the antagonist. The first part is admirable. The second is a common but devastating mistake. Because no matter how interesting you've made your protagonist or how well you've melded character and plot, it's not going to generate much interest unless your character faces some serious opposition.

I realize that not every story can be reduced to "good guy vs. bad guy." Often, women's fiction revolves around conflicts of the heart. The antagonist may be a spouse, lover, or child who is not at all a "bad guy." Literary fiction may focus primarily on internal conflicts and the protagonist may be her own worst enemy. A science fiction novel may put its hero in opposition to a tyrannical society (though these stories typically work better when there is a human representative of the society, such as President Snow in *The Hunger Games* series). But whatever form the antagonist takes and the stronger that antagonism is, the better the book will be.

Let me use one of my favorite series characters, James Bond, as an example. You may know Bond from the fine films, but the books present a much richer, more complex character and considerably more realistic espionage. In the first entry in the series, *Casino Royale*, Bond is posed against a French gambler, Le Chiffre, who's in deep with the Russian assassin group SMERSH. He needs money badly. Bond's task is to beat Le Chiffre at chemin de fer, a gambling game based completely on luck, which involves no real strategy whatsoever. But of course, Bond succeeds. Le Chiffre retaliates with a gruesome torture scene, but nonetheless—he's not much of a challenge for Bond. He's defeated altogether too easily. (The more dramatic action of the book, and what made it powerful, is the action between Bond and his lover, Vesper). So Ian Fleming succeeded in creating a fabulous leading character, the amazingly resourceful multi-talented Bond—but to a large degree failed to create a worthy opponent.

Fleming recognized the problem. From that book forward, the antagonists would increase in power and stature. The world of real-life espionage would be left behind as Bond confronted a long series of megalomaniacs with grandiose objectives. Fantasy figures, to be sure, but much more challenging opponents for Commander Bond.

In the next book, *Live and Let Die*, Bond confronts "Mr. Big," the Harlem kingpin who's the link between laundered antique coins from Russia and the Jamaican drug trade. Mr. Big tortures, maims, and controls a seemingly endless army of operatives. He makes Le Chiffre look like Pepe Le Pew. Future Bond opponents would include Dr. No and Goldfinger, characters so large their names become the titles of the book. None of the books are titled for the hero (unless you count *The Spy Who Loved Me*, a collection of short stories). But these villains are so much larger-than-life that they become title-worthy. Fleming learned his lesson well—and that's one of the key reasons the series has survived so long and so well.

When Arthur Conan Doyle wanted to kill off Sherlock Holmes (a decision he lived to regret), he was faced with a seemingly insurmountable problem. Since he'd created a character so much smarter than anyone else on earth, who could possibly take him down? Retirement seemed unlikely, as did a change of occupation. No, Holmes needed a worthy opponent, someone more challenging than the small-time operators encountered in his previous cases. So Doyle created James Moriarty, a professor of mathematics who, in his secret life, is "the Napoleon of Crime." Could any opponent be bigger than the Napoleon of Crime? Especially to readers in the last part of the nineteenth century?

Even though Holmes's death in "The Final Problem" turns out to be faked (only Moriarty died), this confrontation is the best-loved and best remembered of all the short stories. Why? Because for once, Holmes appears to confront an antagonist worthy of him. Not coincidentally, every modern incarnation of Holmes has seen fit to revive Moriarty, including the Robert Downey, Jr. films, the *Elementary* television series and the BBC *Sherlock* series. Because they all know that drama is at its best when a protagonist faces opposition that is his equal— or perhaps even his superior.

One last example: Superman. Imagine the writer's problem, trying to create a worthy opponent for a guy who basically could destroy the universe just by listening hard. He's got about every power imaginable. How do you create an exciting challenge for him? The first tales penned by teenagers Jerry Siegel and Joe Shuster were basically socialist-crusader stories. Superman never faced any major opposition. He just pummeled wife-beaters and threatened slumlords and saved innocent men from execution (so see, Ben Kincaid really is just like Superman. Or perhaps Clark Kent). But as the series developed, other writers recognized the need to raise the stakes by developing antagonists worthy of the Man of Steel.

The first and probably best-known opponent for the last son of Krypton was Lex Luthor. Lex has no superpowers but he is incredibly intelligent, and that allows him to put the Big Blue Cheese through his paces. As comics gravitated more and more toward "slugfests," that is, titanic city-block-size fistfights between super-powerful beings, a more physically challenging opponent was needed. Now most readers would consider Superman's arch-nemesis Darkseid, an eerie "god" from the planet Apokolips whose powers have never been well defined, but he's scary and he manages to push Superman around. In both the Richard Donner and the Zack Snyder Superman films, they used General Zod, another survivor of the planet Krypton—and therefore someone who can pack a punch just as powerful as the protagonist.

You're probably not writing a comic book, nor am I suggesting that you should. But I am suggesting that you magnify your conflicts with an antagonist who will give your hero extraordinary opposition.

Remember also that just as your protagonist and your plot should be matched, your antagonist and your plot should be matched. This can happen two ways. You can create a villain who causes a problem that your heroine is specially qualified to oppose. Or, if you really want to make life tough for your character (perhaps in the third or fourth volume of a series), create an antagonist who causes problems that your heroine's abilities are completely powerless against. Luthor wearing a Kryptonite ring. Sherlock Holmes misled by a seductive woman. Jean Valjean forced to turn himself in to prevent an innocent man from suffering the same unjust prison sentence he received.

That's how you keep your readers hooked. And once you've got them hooked, you can tell the story you want to tell, conveying your message or theme. And your readers will love every page of it.

Highlights

1) The protagonist's story is only as good as the antagonist makes it.

2) Weak opposition will lead to a weak story.

Red Sneaker Exercises

1) In the last chapter, you considered the pairing of the plot and protagonist. Now consider the pairing of the plot and the antagonist. How can you make your antagonist a more worthy match for your protagonist? How can you make your antagonist just right for the plot you're planning—or the plot just right for the antagonist?

CHAPTER 5: THE THRILL OF SURPRISE

A story to me means a plot where there is some surprise. Because that is how life is—full of surprises.

Isaac Bashevis Singer

What is it that makes readers keep turning the pages of a book? Sure, people like to be entertained by stories. Since the days of primitive man, cavemen sat around the campfire telling stories. We know this because the paintings on the walls of the caves in Lascaux, France, in the Great Hall of the Bulls, tell a story, the tale of the mighty hunter who defended the clan against a horrible beast (in other words, a superhero story). Subsequent civilizations thrilled to the adventures of *Gilgamesh*, *Beowulf*, *The Iliad*, *The Odyssey*, and *the Aeneid*. John Ciardi suggested that this love of language, of stories, defines us as humans. I once heard Isabel Allende say, "I'm a story junkie."

I am, too. I bet you are as well. But today, there are so many different ways to get stories. Audiobooks. Internet. Television. Film. Social media. Even tweets. Why do people keep coming back to books?

I think there are several reasons. First and foremost, books engage the imagination at a profound level that no other medium approaches. When you read a book your brain is actively—not passively—engaged, and in the best books, you're as much a character in the narrative as those on the printed page, because you're seeing the world through their eyes. This allows you to empathize with the character. To feel their pain. To worry when they're in danger. To ache when they're separated from their true love.

And it provides one other advantage.

It gives books an unprecedented ability to surprise.

Sometimes a good movie or play will surprise you as well, but not as often and not as profoundly, because you typically are not as emotionally invested in the characters. But when you're seeing the world through a sympathetic character's eyes in the pages of a book, and he's suddenly shocked and horrified—then so are you. When that character discovers something that creates a profound moment of insight or enlightenment, when they see and understand something they did not before—so does the reader.

And that gives the reader a boost of adrenaline that profoundly increases their enjoyment of the book. And makes it all the more likely that they'll keep reading.

Readers like to be surprised.

Mystery and Revelation

E.M. Forster once wrote, "All good books are mysteries." By that, I don't think he meant the only good novels are whodunits. It think he meant there should be an underlying mystery, something the reader doesn't know but wants very much to find out. Otherwise, why would the reader keep plowing ahead?

In Forster's great novel, *A Passage to India*, the plot revolves around a central mystery: What happened in the cave? All we know for certain is that some people went in, and Adela runs hysterically out, later claiming she was sexually assaulted by Dr. Aziz. Forster's description of the cave episode is particularly cunning and well-written. Employing all five senses, he managed to write a scene that is absolutely terrifying, but gives the reader no certainty about what actually happened.

This book is a work of serious literary fiction, not a whodunit, with pointed commentary about life in India under the British Raj. Nonetheless, the various intrigues and plots and subplots all gravitate around that central mystery: What happened in the cave? And Forster does not answer that question till the very end of the trial, with an explanation that both unites all the other stories—and surprises the reader.

Cheap Thrills

I like to divide plot surprises into two categories: Cheap Thrills and Proper Surprises. Neither is necessarily bad. They can both serve a purpose, if employed skillfully. Ultimately, a well-planted and natural surprise will produce a more lingering, profound reading experience. But as anyone who's ever been on a drag strip in a Corvette convertible knows, cheap thrills are not without pleasure.

Typically, a cheap thrill is completely unexpected. It comes out of nowhere. It has not been planted in advance. It may not be true to the characters. In the worst cases, it may not even be credible (see *Scream 3*). But it is surprising, and we all get a little jolt from being surprised. In *Alien*, in a moment of great tension, the cat, Jonesy, suddenly jumps out from the corner of the screen and screeches. Everyone in the theater jumped. This is not what you would call a profound moment in the history of cinema. But it sure was surprising. It energized the audience—and braced them for the far worse terror to come.

You might get away with one or two of these cheap thrills in your book. But don't do it too often. At some point, it may start to look amateurish, like you don't know how to plant clues properly to prepare readers for a more meaningful surprise, or like you didn't outline your book, so you're just throwing out weird stuff as soon as it pops into your head. Instead, plan for a more natural way to surprise your audience, a cunning twist that no matter how sharp they are, they won't see coming.

Proper Surprises

You've probably heard the term "plot twist." This is probably not the best description for what I'm calling a proper surprise, because it rarely actually represents the plot going off in a different direction. What it does mean is that the reader learns something they didn't know before or experiences something they didn't anticipate. This can inject tremendous energy into your book. In the book on structure, I recommended at least two major plot twists in Act 2, because novels often suffer from middle-of-the-book sag. This is a great way to prevent this from happening.

A good surprise will energize the story.

There are certain requirements to a good surprise. First, it must actually surprise (duh). Second, it must seem organic to the story. Third, the essential clues leading up to it must have been fairly (if inconspicuously) planted. Fourth, it must be credible (not likely, but credible). Fifth, the reader should feel they could have and should have seen it coming—but didn't. Sixth, and this is the big one:

42

PERFECTING PLOT

A great surprise will lend insight to the story.

Let's take each of these requirements point-by-point. I think you probably already grasp that a good surprise should surprise. Easy to say, hard to pull off. When I say it must seem organic to the story, I'm simply saying that it should not seem to come out of nowhere, like the screeching cat leaping from an unseen corner of the screen. You may have heard the famous quote from Anton Chekhov: "If in the first act you have hung a pistol on the wall, then in the following one it should be fired." He's saying, don't build up audience anticipation and then thwart it.

The converse rephrasing of Chekhov's truism is: If there's going to be a pistol fired in Act 3, you'd better plant it in Act 1. And you must do something to make sure the reader remembers what you planted—without cluing them to how important it will be later in the book. If something critical appears out of nowhere, readers will feel it's all too convenient and coincidental (see next chapter), like the iron crowbar that always seems to be just within the reach of the woman being assaulted in the parking garage on cop shows. If, however, you've made a point of establishing that the pistol is on the wall, perhaps for an entirely innocuous reason (Granddad's gift, a show prop, a crime writers' award), then it will not seem coincidental and readers will be delighted to see it put into use.

In *The Hunger Games*, Peeta escapes certain death because, being a baker, he knows how to disguise himself to look like a tree trunk (sometimes it's best to just go with this stuff). Suzanne Collins made a point of establishing earlier in the book that his ability to ice a cake gave him the ability to disguise himself to evade the marauding gangs after he's wounded. If you hadn't been told beforehand that he had this ability, it would've seemed preposterous.

In my book *Extreme Justice*, Ben's friend Mike Morelli, knowing that Ben is physically inept but prone to getting himself into trouble, insists that he study jiu jitsu. Ben reluctantly agrees. He only attends one lesson and performs like the klutz he is. But he does manage to learn one move, an over-the-shoulder flip.

Several hundred pages later, in the final moments of the climax, guess what saves his life?

You've got the idea. If something is going to be critical to the success of your surprise, make sure it's been planted in advance. In the Golden Age of mysteries, the era of Agatha Christie and Ellery Queen, people talked about "fair play" mysteries. The idea was that all the essential clues were presented to the reader, just as they were to the detective, so the reader had an equal chance of solving the mystery. This, of course, almost never happened. Because a good mystery writer knows how to present information without making it seem like a clue. A passing line of dialogue. A random bit of description. An offhand joke. But never: "Gosh," the detective pondered, "I wonder if that's important." Because you don't want the reader to even consider the possibility. You just want them to remember that the later-to-be important detail was mentioned.

The degree of credibility your surprise requires will depend upon the degree of realism in your story. Here's what I can say for certain: Within the context of the universe you've created, it must seem plausible. If you've written about a world with flying cars and ray guns, then an assassination from a flying car with a ray gun is plausible. If your book is set in 2013, it isn't. Cozy mysteries are sometimes more accepting of elaborate murder schemes, because the fun of the book doesn't derive from the realism but from the cleverness of the detection. Romances may not care whether the pairing is likely but only whether the couple seems happy together. You have to do what's right for your book.

Both of these last two elements unite to determine whether the reader will feel they should've or could've seen this surprise coming. If it was clued properly and seems credible within the world you've created, it should give them the happy feeling that they've been fooled by a masterful writer.

Will Your Surprise Work?

You can never be certain whether a surprise will work, because all readers are not alike. As with most aspects of writing, there are no guarantees. Let's consider a few famous examples.

Fight Club is a terrific novel by one of my favorite writers, Chuck Palahniuk, which was also made into a fine film. The story itself is riveting, but what everyone talks about is the ending—the big surprise. If, like me, you loved the surprise, thought it had been fairly planted, and was an insanely clever bit of writing, you enjoyed it. But some people didn't. I recall hearing Rosie O'Donnell on the air, advising people not to see the movie because she thought the ending was a "rip-off."

Like I said, people are different. Some people feel fooled or tricked when the author pulls the wool over their eyes. But I appreciate cleverness, I like reading authors who are smarter than me, and I loved every minute of it.

Let's consider another example, this time from the world of film. Many of you may be fans of M Night Shyamalan's file *The Sixth Sense*. I thought the film rather slow-paced, revolving around a small boy who can "see dead people," but even after Bruce Willis figures this out, he doesn't do much with it. Anyway, without spoiling anything for the uninitiated, the vast popularity of this film and its water-cooler buzz revolves around the big surprise at the ending. I did not see it coming. I did get a buzz when it was revealed.

But I didn't feel it was fairly planted, and that spoiled it for me. Only a little. But still.

Yes, they replay clips from earlier in the film from a different perspective to show you why you "should have realized" all along what was really happening. But I still felt the clues weren't there and I had been misled. Most of Shyamalan's subsequent films have revolved around a similar big surprise at the end, each one weaker than the one before.

I think the message here is that, while a big satisfying surprise can energize a book, it can't be the only appeal of a book. You still have to tell a good story.

Illumination

The best surprises will illuminate the story and cause readers to see everything in a different way than they did before.

The ideal plot development will not only balloon the reader's eyes but also illuminate the preceding narrative. Perhaps it explains a character contradiction the reader did not understand before. Perhaps it explains a mysterious plot point introduced in the prologue but never explained.

But in some way it not only galvanizes the reader but provides a feeling of revelation.

In other words, you don't want a plot twist that causes the reader to say, "Huh? What? That doesn't make any sense."

You want the reader to slap his hand against his forehead and say, "Of course! Now it all makes sense."

To me, the best example of this is Ian McEwan's extraordinary novel *Atonement*.

My biggest challenge in this chapter is to discuss a big surprise without giving away the big surprise. But trust me, this book has a big one. And this is serious literary fiction by one of the best writers of the century. The entire book is riveting. Beautifully crafted prose by a master of the English language. But oh my, the ending…

Some critics felt the surprise invalidated too much of what they had spent their time reading. Those critics, forgive me for saying, completely missed the point. McEwan planted the necessary information and set up the twist perfectly, starting with the title itself. The ending is about the lead character's atonement. It's breathtakingly surprising and so much more. It quite literally explains everything that has gone before. It knocks the top of your head off, to quote Emily Dickinson. The lead character is a writer, and it brilliantly illuminates the writer's work, the writer's motivation—and the writer's unending dilemma.

McEwan is always superb, but *Atonement* put him in the highest echelon of contemporary literary figures. And if you can come up with an illuminating surprise that powerful, you might end up in the same pantheon.

Surprise vs. Stupidity

Is it possible to go too far with the surprises? Of course it is. You've probably read books where almost every chapter ends with some major game-changing surprise, each a little more unlikely than the one before. As with anything else, excessive repetition leads to diminished impact.

If you can put two really strong unexpected proper surprises in your book, you've done well. And placement is everything. As I've said, surprises in the middle may help bolster a sagging middle. But you may've also noticed that in Harlan Coben's wonderful thrillers, there's often a major surprise revealed quite literally on the last page (check out *Tell No One*, for one example). Talk about going out with a bang. If you can end your book with a big head-thunking surprise that causes the reader to realize something they didn't know, that explains some detail they'd forgotten about, that illuminates the action of the entire book, I can just about guarantee readers will be talking about your book with their friends. All of *Tell No One* is excellent, but more than anything else, I think it's the last page that transformed Harlan Coben from a little known cozy mystery writer to one of the most prominent thriller writers working today.

But like anything else, it's possible to push a good thing too far. You can have too many surprises, and you can also reach the point where your surprises simply push people's credibility beyond their limits. Some people felt that way about the end of *The Da Vinci Code* (I didn't). Some people felt that way about *Fight Club* (I didn't). And some people felt that way about Clive Cussler's Dirk Pitt novel, *Sahara*.

Cussler literally reinvented the modern thriller, hitting the lists with *Raise the Titanic* and remaining there ever since. What may surprise you is that he's also a fine prose stylist, a student of Hemingway who learned his lessons and in many ways even improved upon them. I know Clive and I've had several fascinating conversations with him discussing many topics, including the one I'm approaching now, so I hope he will forgive me if I take small fault with *Sahara*.

For the uninitiated, Cussler employs a high-octane macho series character named Dirk Pitt whose abilities border on the superhuman. This book leads him and a few cohorts on an intriguing adventure which eventually brings them, as you may have already guessed, to the Sahara. It's a desperate situation. They're surrounded by well-armed villains. And then they discover something buried in the sand.

A submarine.

Yes, you read me right. And if you don't think that's quite surprising enough—it's a Civil War submarine. From the American Civil War. *The CSS Texas.*

Turns out there's been some shifting in the gulf stream, and what was once a waterway is now a desert, and that's why there's a submarine there. Okay, fine, I like a good surprise.

Guess what they discover next? Some of the sub's weaponry is still operational. They can use it against the bad guys.

At this point, surprise is starting to give way to impossibility. Remember the part about the surprise requiring credibility? We're losing that here. But unfortunately, we're not even done with the surprises yet. Guess what else they find on the sub?

A corpse. Specifically: the corpse of Abraham Lincoln.

Well, that *was* surprising. But for me, it was surprising to the point of being completely unbelievable.

In case history buffs are confused, it turns out that the kindly gentleman assassinated in Ford's Theater was actually an actor hired to impersonate Lincoln. White House intelligence had obtained hints of a plan to kidnap Lincoln, so they used this doppelganger for public appearances. The plan apparently didn't work so well, though, because Southern spies still managed to kidnap the real Lincoln and smuggle him out of Washington in a sub...which eventually ended up in the Sahara. With functioning weapons. Just when Dirk Pitt needed them. (I noticed that when the film adaptation was made, they left in the sub, but eliminated the part about Lincoln's skeletal remains.)

Don't get me wrong—*Sahara* is still a fun book. But I do think it's an example of the author's desire to surprise exceeding credibility to the point that the surprise just isn't fun anymore. Don't let this discourage you from planning surprises. Just make sure they follow the guidelines I outlined. It's a wonderful way to delight your readers—and illuminate the character and the story at the same time.

PERFECTING PLOT

Highlights

1) Readers like to be surprised.

2) A good surprise will energize the story.

3) A great surprise lends insight to the story.

4) The best surprises illuminate the story and cause the reader to see everything in a different way than they did before.

5) A good surprise should be surprising, organic to the main plot, well planted, fairly foreshadowed, and illuminating.

6) If surprises occur too frequently, they lose impact.

7) Some surprises are so outrageous and unlikely that the credibility problem outweighs whatever pleasure might've been obtained from the surprise.

Red Sneaker Exercises

1) I hope by this time you have a working outline of your book. Look through the outline and see if you've got some good, unexpected, illuminating surprises planned (particularly in Act 2).

2) When the surprise is revealed, how will your readers see your main character, or the story, differently than they did before?

3) Consider how to plant the necessary clues to foreshadow your surprises without tipping off the reader. Disguise it as something innocuous: party banter, idle conversation, or a passing description.

CHAPTER 6: THE AGONY OF COINCIDENCE

It is such a complex matter we live within, it is impossible to track logic and decision-making really, so therefore each choice can actually only be seen as coincidence.

Alva Noto

Having just heard me rattle on about the power of surprise, you may be startled to now read me criticizing coincidence. Isn't coincidence just another form of surprise?

In a word: no. Coincidence is a plotting flaw, one that can quite literally destroy your book.

Remember when I told you readers love surprises? Here's the converse:

Readers hate coincidence.

The Problem with Coincidence

Some early writers may have difficulty distinguishing between a surprise and a coincidence, because after all, isn't all this plot just stuff we're making up? Yes, but some ways of making stuff up are better than others, which is basically the overall topic of this book.

Other writers may wonder why there should be antithesis toward coincidence when our real lives are filled with astonishing coincidences. How many of you have been sitting around thinking about an old friend—and then that very friend calls you for the first time in twenty years? Or perhaps an unexpected paycheck arrives just when you're on the verge of being flat broke. Or exactly the book you need suddenly falls off the shelf into your lap.

In truth, there may be logical reasons for these coincidences. You and your old friend may have both read the same magazine article, which triggered the same memory, resulting in the phone call. Your debtor may have heard you were having tough times and decided it was time to pay the debt. There may be logical explanations for all these occurrences, but they seem unexplained and amazing. One of the reasons many some believe in ESP—despite the absence of any scientific evidence whatsoever—is that these amazing events occur, and people can't think of any other explanation. It's easier to think, "You must've read my mind," than "We must've read the same magazine article."

At any rate, this is my way of reminding you that while novels should have verisimilitude, it's not the job of the novelist to reproduce reality. In reality, coincidence occurs all the times, so often no one thinks much about it. "Small world, isn't it?" people say, when these startling coincidences arise.

But in novels, readers hate coincidence because it reminds them that the story isn't real. It disturbs the seeming relationship between cause and effect you've constructed. It reminds readers that there's a writer concocting all this, when they want to be immersed in the story, not you.

Now perhaps you understand why earlier I used the term "proper surprises." A coincidence is an unnatural surprise, and unwanted, too. Coincidence is not only the use of the shotgun that wasn't planted, but the deliverance of the shotgun into the hands of the hero by the sudden appearance of a previously undetected black hole disrupting the fabric of the space-time continuum.

Coincidence may be commonplace in real life, but when it happens in a novel, it makes the reader feel the book is unrealistic. This is another reason it's so important to plant the clues to your surprises, so they seem to arise naturally, rather than coincidentally.

Novels thrive on an imagined sense of cause and effect. Even though Einsteinian physics tells us that when time is warped, effect can actually precede cause, most people expect it to happen the other way around. When you plant your clue, your shotgun, whatever else it is, you've established cause. Therefore, it seems natural when the effect occurs later. Coincidence is effect without cause, which seriously disturbs the reader's pleasure in the book. It makes it seem as if this hasn't happened because the story is unfolding naturally, but rather, because that's the way the writer wants it to happen. In other words, instead of seeing the development of the characters and the natural evolution of the plot, they see the hand of the writer.

And they don't want to see the hand of the writer.

Nothing against your hand, which I'm sure is lovely. But when a reader is in the midst of a novel, they want to be absorbed in the story. They want to forget the rest of the world exists, outside the troubled lives of the viewpoint character and the rest of the cast. You may have heard the expression, "You must kill your darlings." This is why. You may have devised a breathtakingly beautiful turn of phrase, so lovely it causes readers to catch their breath and think about what a fabulous writer you are. But unfortunately, you've drawn them out of the story, and you may never get back in again.

You want them thinking about the story, not the author. After the book is done, and you've thrilled them or brought them to tears, then, after they've caught their breath, they can turn to your author photo on the back flap and think, "Wow. She is a tremendous writer." But not before. When they're in the midst of a story, leave them there. Don't rely on coincidence, which will only make the reader see the hand of the author moving the characters around like pieces on a chessboard.

Deus ex machina

Some of you may recall a discussion in English class of the principle of *deus ex machina*, a term derived from Greek theater that roughly translated means "the machine of the gods." This plot device represents coincidence at its highest (and worst) form. In the ancient Greeks' primitive stagecraft, a crank-and-lever contraption would literally raise an actor playing a god from below the stage through a trap door. The god would then use his magical powers to fix all the problems of the play.

Can you see where modern audiences might find that less than satisfying? A supernatural entity coincidentally appearing just when he's needed? I'm not even sure this worked well for the ancient Greeks. Here's a fact: starting around the fourth century B.C., it's believed that several thousand Greek plays utilized the *deus ex machina* plot device, many of them written by major playwrights. How many have survived?

Maybe seven.

PERFECTING PLOT

Thomas Hardy has also been criticized for excessive dependence upon coincidence. I'm a huge fan of Hardy's work. I think he's one of the greatest novelists of his era and a fine poet, too. But there is that nagging problem of coincidence.

Do you remember the tragic *Tess of the D'Urbervilles*? Do you recall how Tess confesses her past sins in a note she slides under Angel Clare's door? When he remains affectionate to her the next day, she thinks he's forgiven her. Only much later does she learn that the note went under the doormat and he never saw it. Do you recall *The Mayor of Casterbridge*, perhaps Hardy's greatest work...and the letter that gets lost for twenty years, only to be discovered by Henchard on Elizabeth-Jane's wedding day, informing him that Elizabeth-Jane is not his biological daughter. While Hardy's reliance upon coincidence did not destroy these fine books, it did not enhance them, either.

In another classic novel, Thornton Wilder's *The Bridge of San Luis Rey*, the author tells the story of five people who died when the same bridge collapsed. If these five were related in some way, say, they were all members of the same fraternity, or they all participated in the same murder, this might seem too coincidental. In this case, however, the five characters have no overt link. They simply die together. In flashback, the author tells their pre-death stories. The end result is almost the opposite of coincidence. The author is showing how cruelly random life can be. Some of the characters' lives were happy, some sad. Some lived fine lives, some lived terrible lives. But they all died together, in the same purposeless, meaningless accident. The author is not relying on coincidence. He's making a point about the illusion of destiny and our tenuous existence.

Permit me one example from the world of film, first because it's a good example and second, because I haven't referred to *Star Trek* in this book yet.

The first J.J. Abrams-directed *Star Trek* film, the reboot, was a marvelous adventure. Abrams may not have captured the philosophical underpinnings that distinguished *Trek* from other SF, but he told a rip-snorting adventure story. A renegade Romulan from the future, Nero, travels back in time to settle a serious grudge. In his first appearance, he destroys a spaceship, but only after Kirk's father takes command of the ship and buys the rest of the crew time to evacuate, sacrificing himself.

Then Nero disappears for twenty-five years.

And when does he return? When Kirk, Jr., our hero, makes his first sojourn out on a spaceship.

Now that is quite a coincidence.

Watching the film the first time, I thought, Ah, Nero must be trying to eradicate Kirk, the great Federation warrior, from the timeline. But no, actually it turns out to be a vendetta against Spock. The repeated appearances of the Kirk family are just coincidence. And let's not even get into the business of the exiled Kirk being randomly torpedoed to the same planet occupied by the alternate-universe Spock *and* Scotty. I might've let it go if Kirk had just been sent to the same planet. But chased into the same cave? Way too coincidental for this Trekkie.

Did these coincidences destroy the movie? (To be fair, a not-very-good-explanation for Nero's twenty-five year disappearance was cut from the final film—because it was a not-very-good explanation). Opinions will differ. But a good writer will learn to spot those coincidences in advance and improve on them by coming up with a surprise or plot development that seems more natural—

because it has been properly foreshadowed and planted. With a little script tinkering, Nero could have been on a vendetta against the Kirk lineage. Tess's note could have been hidden by a well-meaning relative. This is another good reason for preplanning and outlining—so you don't find yourself trapped in a plot box that can only be advanced or resolved with a coincidence.

Highlights

1) Readers hate coincidence

2) Avoid *deus ex machina* endings in which the plot is resolved by something that has not been foreshadowed and seems all too convenient.

Red Sneaker Exercises

1) Review the outline for your story. Each scene should describe an event that causes a change in a character's situation as a result of conflict. Now consider how those changes occur. Are they a natural result of what has happened before? Or do they seem coincidental?

2) If you find scenes in your book in which you fear the revelations will seem coincidental, consider how to plant foreshadowing earlier in the book to avoid that problem. Perhaps a previously established course of conduct that an antagonist can exploit. A weakness or vulnerability established well before it becomes important to the plot. Something that will make the event seem more natural and less convenient.

3) Coincidence is never welcome, but the point where it can be most deadly is the climax. This is why you should avoid *deus ex machina* resolutions. However your hero triumphs, regardless of what device he uses to do it, make sure it's something that was planted long before— and if it isn't, rewrite your outline immediately. In the climax, you want your readers to feel a surge of enthusiasm

due to your hero's resourcefulness, not to roll their eyes and think, "Well, isn't that convenient."

WILLIAM BERNHARDT

CHAPTER 7: LAYERING THE CONFLICT

The greatest rules of dramatic writing are conflict, conflict, and conflict.

James Frey

Throughout this book I've discussed the importance of conflict. Conflict is what makes your story tick, what makes the plot move forward, and what keeps readers turning pages (or tapping the edge of their eReader). But it's important to understand that there are many different kinds of conflict, and as a writer, you must be able to distinguish among them, so you can determine which will be right for your book. You may choose to use one rather than the other. You may even choose to use them all. But you can't do that unless you understand what they are.

In his Nobel Prize acceptance speech, William Faulkner described his work as being about "the human heart in conflict with itself," which is perhaps the only thing worth writing about. This chapter is about how to layer that kind of emotional conflict into your work—while also telling a compelling story.

The Three Layers of Conflict

Conflict can be inner, personal, or external.

I find it useful to divide conflict into these three categories, though it will probably soon be evident that you could create additional subdivisions for each of them. But here's general breakdown:

Inner conflicts are those taking place in your protagonist's head. Fear. Dread. Neurosis. Mental illness. Fear of aging. Self-loathing. Inability to commit. Laziness. Gullibility. The need to be loved. Moral dilemmas. The people around them may not even be aware that your characters are suffering these conflicts. But they are in fact suffering.

Personal conflicts revolve around relationships with others. If inner conflicts are matters of the head, then personal conflicts are matters of the heart. What does your protagonist want more than anything else in the world? What does her heart desire most? Love. Sex. Romance. Approval of parents. Security for children. Success for friends. These conflicts will be much more readily apparent to other characters and to the reader.

External conflicts put your protagonist in opposition to a powerful force in the outside world. In many books, this will be the primary conflict, though elements of the others may be present. This is your protagonist doing battle with the many faces of adversity in the world—the serial killer, the deadly robot, the corrupt corporate officials, the person or institution that prevents lovers from coming together.

PERFECTING PLOT

Inner Conflict

Few novels survive strictly on inner conflict, though some have tried. In the modernist era of the early twentieth century, several writers experimented with a form of writing called "stream of consciousness" (a term actually borrowed from the psychologist William James, Henry's brother). The idea is that the focus is on the thoughts occurring within a character's head, which in some cases may drift from one character's head to another. There are few successful examples of this, and even those are primary successful for English majors, not those looking for riveting reading. Virginia Woolf did it best, in *To the Lighthouse* and *Mrs. Dalloway*, though Faulkner's *The Sound and the Fury* is also an extraordinary achievement. A more recent example that many readers admired was *Omensetter's Luck* by William H. Gass.

Those who read my book on character will recall the more detailed discussion of *Hamlet*. Suffice to say that although this play is rife with conflict, that conflict is almost entirely internal. Should I kill my uncle? Should I kill him now or wait until later? Could I trick him into confessing? Not until the last scenes of the play does any true action occur

Inner conflict is not about the war fought on the streets or the battlefield but the war raging within. And this war will be at its most dramatic when your character confronts two choices, both of which have negative consequences. Don't make it a choice between good or evil. Most readers are savvy enough to know how that's going to come out. Make it a choice between alternatives that both have advantages but also inescapable (or so it seems) negative consequences.

Inner conflict is not the same as inner turmoil. Suffering is a static condition. It is not dynamic, and it is not conflict. And frankly, most readers have a low threshold for characters who sit around wringing their hands. Look for ways to create external manifestations of the conflict brewing within.

If you're having trouble coming up with a good inner struggle for your character, I've made a long list of them and attached it as Appendix A. Comb through the list and see if it triggers any ideas you can use. Sometimes the inner conflict can represent an inner fear, flaw, or shortcoming. The devious writer will exploit this problem by constructing a plot that forces that character to go wherever they would least like to go. The protagonist's eventual triumph over this failing can represent a primary or secondary character arc.

Regardless of what inner conflict you choose, push your protagonists to their furthest limit. That's how we overcome our fears—by confronting them. Maybe your readers will have a vicarious reading experience that allows them to overcome their fears as well.

Personal Conflict

If your book thrives solely on personal conflicts, than you have a melodrama, or what some might call a "soap opera," a term becoming increasingly dated. It's also increasingly inaccurate, because most so-called soap operas or nighttime soaps also have external conflicts. They just don't come to the forefront. The primary conflict will involve who loves who, who doesn't, who secretly loves who but won't admit it, who once loved someone and lost her and now would do anything to get her back...and so forth. Romance novels might also fit in this category, although most modern romance novels are so much more sophisticated that I'm unwilling to categorize them by a single characteristic.

Sometimes people have trouble coming up with a good personal conflict that isn't just another trite love story, so I've attached a list of possibilities in Appendix B. Again, not an exhaustive list, but some possibilities. And depending upon the type of book you're writing, some of them also might work as or in addition to your external conflict. Don't use them all, please. Your goal is to make your readers want to read your book, not to make them want to shoot themselves in the head.

Sometimes aspiring writers will hear that they need a personal conflict, so they add a girlfriend and think the job is done. Wrong. The job is just beginning. Okay, your protagonist has a romantic partner, but so what? And don't try to create conflict with some easy obvious plot point, like, they had a spat. They're growing apart. He's not home enough. He forgot her anniversary. Are we really supposed to care?

You can find a way to make the personal conflict more interesting. Instead of just a run-of-the-mill girlfriend, what if she's the lover with whom he had the best sex of his life but hasn't seen for twenty years, until suddenly she moves into his apartment building—just after he proposed to his fiancé? What if he's a lonely widower who can't get over the loss of his wife of forty-five years...and one day the woman at the supermarket checkout counter starts flirting with him?

Dig deeper. There is nothing on earth more complex than human relationships, so you have a wealth of material from which to draw. Find something that reads true but is still unique. Fill your personal conflicts with surprises, unexpected events from the past or future, and ideally, developments that enhance the reader's understanding of the characters involved.

External Conflict

If your book revolves around external conflict, you're probably writing an action-adventure story, or to use a hipper term, a "thriller." As the name might suggest, a thriller must thrill, and that happens when the protagonist is opposed by seemingly overwhelming odds. They might be fighting a villain. They might be fighting the conventions of society. They might be fighting the government. But they are fighting something external to themselves in an effort to make their world a better place, if not to save it altogether.

The most important factor to remember about external conflict is to make it big. That doesn't mean there has to be a ticking time bomb or that the world must be on the brink of destruction. It does mean that the conflict must be important to the protagonist and perhaps to others as well. Whether you're writing literary fiction or popular fiction, if the external conflict seems trivial, readers will lose interest rapidly.

Here's another tip for devising your external conflict: The best will be an external reflection of the inner conflict.

Turn that core conflict inside out.

Action scenes are always going to be more powerful than internal monologue, though both can be used skillfully. So perhaps the protagonist's sins of the past, that which creates his inner conflict, many years later create an external conflict of larger proportions. Perhaps the hero learns that he and the villain both suffered the same pain, and the external conflict is magnified by the fact that they turn out to be much more alike than they are different. Batman and his arch-nemesis, the Joker, were both psychologically damaged at an early age. They're just dealing with it in decidedly different ways. So in terms of external conflict, Batman is trying to save Gotham, and the Joker is trying to destroy it—but both urges stem from the same inner conflict.

Since I've discussed how the different levels of conflict can be related, you may be wondering: Can I use more than one? Of course you can. Each additional layer of conflict will enrich your story.

Here's a crazy idea: Why not use all three?

If you do, you'll have the best story possible, one that might work on so many different levels simultaneously that your reader can't put the down and talks about it long after they've finished reading it

Stacking Conflict

In most cases, coming up with your protagonist's inner conflict may be the easiest part of this process. You probably had some understanding of who this character was from the outset, and that includes understanding their struggles and issues. Your protagonist wants something— that's what moves the story forward—and something prevents her from getting it. But is it possible that in addition to the external or antagonist-based opposition, there are inner demons that prevent your character's success? Dan Brown's Robert Langdon struggles with claustrophobia. He can face down the ominous Opus Dei, but he can't ride an elevator without getting sweaty. Ben

Kincaid can give a great closing argument but he can't talk to girls. Batman can take down supervillains but he's haunted by the loss of his parents—survivor's guilt. In the initial adventures, C.S. Forester's great naval hero, Horatio Hornblower, suffers from seasickness, which makes him fear failure. Inner conflicts will not detract from your character's heroism. To the contrary, they will enhance it. Remember the famous quote often attributed to John Wayne: "Real courage is being scared to death but saddling up anyway."

Let's say you want to make your story richer (because you do). Now that you've got an interesting protagonist struggling with a powerful inner conflict, let's add a personal conflict. The most common one, of course, is a love interest. Many thrillers have added a subplot romance (Hitchcock, almost always after *The 39 Steps*) that has little the do with the main story but perhaps will broaden the appeal to those who aren't all that interested in the running and jumping and shooting. But that's not your only choice. Many serious novels have revolved around conflicts with parents, or parents having conflicts with their children. Ivan Turgenev's aptly titled *Fathers and Sons*. Larry McMurtry's *Terms of Endearment*. W.P. Kinsella's *Shoeless Joe* (which became the film *Field of Dreams*). Why are these conflicts so common in stories? The answer should be obvious: Because they're so common in real life.

And then there is the external conflict. If you're writing a mystery or thriller, you may have thought about this part first. Sometimes in an action-adventure story, the whole novel seems to gravitate around the power struggle between good guy and bad guy—and sadly, in some cases, that's about all there is. But not in the best ones. Not in the ones that resonate in your memory.

PERFECTING PLOT

There have been a million monster movies. Why do we remember *Jaws* so fondly? Because it was about so much more than three guys chasing a shark. The protagonist is Sheriff Brody, who left NYC for a better place to raise his family, trying to prove himself in a small coastal town (inner conflict). He has personal conflicts with his wife and his children (in the Benchley novel, she's having an affair). And of course, there's the hunt for the great white, which—speaking of conflict—forces Brody to team up with shark expert Quint—whom he strongly dislikes.

In *Dark Eye*, Susan faces conflict on all fronts. Inner conflict: she must battle her addiction. Personal conflict: She's trying to reestablish her relationship with her niece, her only surviving relative. External conflict: She has to catch a maniacal killer.

Conflict, conflict, conflict.

For me perhaps the greatest example of layering conflict is in Mark Twain's classic *The Adventures of Huckleberry Finn*. You may remember the critical scene in the middle of the book (the character turning point, to borrow a term from structure). At the outset of the book, Huck is put into the hands of Widow Douglas, a strong-willed, religious woman who tries to "sivilize" him. They don't get along so well, and Huck eventually flees with Jim, a slave belonging to one of the Widow's friends, Miss Watson. I don't think Huck dislikes the Widow. In fact, never having had a mother figure in his life before, I suspect he loves her.

In this crisis scene in the middle of the novel, Huck has been guilted into writing a letter to Miss Watson telling her where she can find her slave. According to what the Widow taught him, by helping Jim escape, Huck has not only committed a crime, but a sin, and sinners go to hell and suffer eternal damnation.

Huck doesn't want to disappoint this woman he cares about, this woman kind enough to take him into her own home. And after the *Dred Scot* decision, slaves were legally determined to be property. Helping a slave— property with legs—escape was no different than taking someone's barnyard mule, in the eyes of the law. A felony offense. A crime for which you could be incarcerated. Given these facts, Huck's most personally advantageous course of action should seem obvious.

But there's a problem. Huck has spent a lot of time on the road with Jim. He's gotten to know him, not as a slave, but as a person. Jim seems no different from all the other people Huck has known. When he looked into Jim's face, his brown eyes seemed no different from Huck's blue ones. So why is it Huck can run free, and Jim is forced to perform slave labor against his will for no compensation?

Huck has never had a day of education in his life. But this doesn't seem right. In fact, it seems very, very wrong. Instinctively wrong.

Inner conflict: Huck doesn't want to be a sinner. Personal conflict: He doesn't want to disappoint his mentor. External conflict: He doesn't want to become a fugitive from the law.

But a voice in his head tells him that slavery is wrong. And so, in the most dramatic scene in this great American novel, he rips the letter up and says, "All right then, I'll go to hell!"

But he won't send Jim back into slavery.

That's how the layering of conflict can take a simple scene and turn it into something beautiful. Huck's rejection of slavery symbolically reflects our own rejection of slavery as a nation, which is why many, including Hemingway, called *Huck Finn* "the greatest American novel."

Conflict in Space

Did you really think you were going to get out of this book with only one *Star Trek* example? How little you know me. Let's consider the pinnacle of the genre, the permanent proof that a sequel is not always inferior to the original: *Star Trek II: The Wrath of Khan*. You probably know the basic story. After a struggle in the original television series, Kirk leaves Khan and his superhuman friends on another planet where they can build their own society (without trying to take over the Federation).

The movie takes place fifteen years later. A supernova turned Khan's Earthlike planet into desert hellhole, killing most of Khan's friends—including his wife. Khan is bitter about this. He's Captain Ahab. (In fact, if you freeze-frame the film when they're in Khan's desert headquarters, you'll see a copy of *Moby Dick* on the bookshelf.) Khan wants revenge against Kirk, the man who abandoned him on that planet. He wants Kirk to suffer as he did. So he escapes, steals a starship, and comes after Kirk, destroying everyone and everything in his path.

Needless to say, that's the external conflict. Kirk must stop Khan.

But as so often happens in fiction, the crisis arises at a most inopportune time. The film opens on a very special day—Kirk's birthday. Specifically, his fiftieth birthday. Spock's gift is an antique book (*A Tale of Two Cities*), and Dr. McCoy gives him something more practical.

Reading glasses.

Movies, let's remember, are a visual medium, and there could be no more potent visual reminder of aging than giving the great macho Klingon-fighter a pair of reading glasses.

Inner conflict: Kirk must face the fact that he's not as young as he used to be (a savvy choice of inner conflict, since the actors playing the roles were obviously not as young as they used to be). And what happens when you get older? You don't move as fast as you once did. You don't think as fast as you once did. And your friends start to die.

Kirk says, "Gallivanting around the cosmos is a young man's game." Later he admits, "I've never faced death. I've lied, cheated, tricked my way out of it. But I've never faced it."

That's about to change.

We need a personal conflict, and that arrives in the form of Kirk's former flame, Carol Marcus. Carol is a research scientist at an outpost that Khan attacks. And she's assisted by her twenty-something son, David.

Guess who the baby daddy is?

We had never previously been told that Kirk had a son. I don't know why we should be surprised. That man probably has kids all across the galaxy. But as you might guess, father and son don't get along well. Kirk wasn't around when the boy was growing up. He was traipsing all across the universe having adventures. And being a scientist, David obviously takes more after his mother's side of the family. David calls his father "an overgrown boy scout." So now we have a personal conflict, one of the oldest known to man, one that stretches back to Biblical times: the conflict between a father and his son.

In the climax and denouement, all these conflicts are resolved, though at a terrible cost. Khan goes down in flames spouting lines stolen from Melville's Captain Ahab ("To the last I grapple with thee; from hell's heart I stab at thee."). Kirk defeats Khan—the external conflict is resolved—but at a terrible cost. Khan detonates "the Genesis device" just before he dies, which will act as a bomb and obliterate Kirk's ship. "Scotty, I need warp drive in three minutes or we're all dead." Only one person can withstand the terrible radiation and enter the warp core chamber: Spock. He succeeds and saves the ship—but dies in the process.

So Kirk has to face aging in the worst possible way. He has to face the death of his best friend. He sits alone in his quarters reading the book Spock gave him, eventually realizing that self-sacrifice like Spock's is a triumph, not a tragedy. ("It is a far, far better thing that I do than I have ever done; it is a far, far better rest that I go to than I have ever known.")

Remember the personal conflict? While Kirk is reading, David knocks on his door, steps inside and says, haltingly, "I just wanted you to know…that I'm proud to be your son." And the two awkwardly embrace.

The personal conflict is resolved.

Energized by the words in the book Spock gave him and the reconciliation with his son, Kirk returns to the bridge. His shipmates are concerned. Carol asks, "How do you feel?"

And Kirk stares out into the vastness of space and says, "I feel young."

The inner conflict is resolved.

I hope you also noticed that, although there are three levels of conflict, they are not completely separate or unrelated, as if they were randomly drawn out of a fishbowl filled with conflict, or generated by one of those ridiculous plot-generating software programs floating around the Internet. Kirk's major problem is aging. So it seems entirely organic that the external conflict should arise from the past, from a mistake he made fifteen years ago. Or that the personal conflict should arise from another mistake he made in the past, a child he fathered but did a poor and inattentive job of raising.

Some of you may be wondering why I have laboriously analyzed conflict in the context of what is basically space opera, a well-made Saturday morning matinee. Here's what I want you to understand: there have been twelve *Star Trek* movies to date, hundreds of television episodes, and there will likely be more in the future.

But this is the best one. By far.

Why? I believe it's because the writer and director, Nicholas Meyer, took the time to layer all these well-conceived and interrelated conflicts together. The film works just fine as an action-adventure outing, a popcorn entertainment. But for the attentive adult viewer, there's more to it than just that. What father's eyes did not itch when David told his father of his pride? I cried like a baby. What older person didn't feel a burst of energy when the aging Kirk, who has just been through so much tragedy, looks out at the viewscreen and says, "I feel young." By layering your conflicts, you give your book additional resonance. More depth. More for the reader to take away with them after the story ends. That's what creates word-of-mouth. And word-of-mouth is what creates bestsellers.

Conflict is the heart and soul of story. The best favor you can do for yourself as a writer is to take the time to think about, plan, outline, write, and rewrite your conflicts until you have them all exactly as they should be.

Until you have three levels of conflict. Until they all relate to one another. Until they are all as powerful as they can possibly be.

Highlights

1) Conflict can be inner, personal, or eternal.

2) Inner conflicts take place in your protagonist's head.

3) Personal conflicts involve relationships with others.

4) External conflicts put your protagonist in opposition to a powerful force in the outside world.

5) The best stories will have all three levels of conflict, and at some level, all three will relate to one another.

Red Sneaker Exercises

1) Earlier I asked you to define your protagonist's primary goal or desire. Now let's complicate that. Can you define what your character wants on three different levels? What is his ultimate quest, that is, what external dragon must he slay? Then, is there a personal relationship that needs to be addressed (and don't add a love interest if you're not going to take the time to adequately develop it)? Finally, what is your character's inner conflict? How is his human heart in conflict with itself?

2) What are your protagonist's personal demons? Is he afraid of heights (*Vertigo*)? Claustrophobia (*The Da Vinci Code*)? Girls (*The Perks of Being a Wallflower*)? Kryptonite? Is

this demon based upon fear? (They usually are.) Where does this fear come from? Is it possible that the resolution of the inner conflict will involve your character finally confronting that fear and overcoming it?

WILLIAM BERNHARDT

CHAPTER 8: UNDERSTANDING YOUR PLOT

The story is not in the plot but in the telling.

Ursula K. LeGuin

Perhaps the question I receive most frequently from students is: How do you fill all those pages? And my answer, of course, is that it's easy (that's a lie, it's never easy) if you understand your plot. Understanding your plot is critical. And that doesn't just mean knowing who are the good guys and who are the bad guys (though those are useful things to know). It means understanding the shape of your story. The plot you're telling.

This can become particularly tricky when people are asked to write a synopsis. Even now, when most submissions are transmitted online, editors and agents usually ask for synopses, either to use to sell the book or to use as a "cheat sheet" in-house for those who don't have time to read the entire book. I know writing these can be difficult, so I've attached some guidelines on writing synopses in Appendix D. But the bottom line is, you can't decide what to include and what to omit from your synopsis until you understand the shape of your plot.

Today the failure to understand the function of plot occurs most frequently in fantasy literature. I don't say that because I'm a snob. I love fantasy. But I think the genre has become so consumed with the artistic or commercial desire to write multi-book epics that some have forgotten the need to properly structure the hero's journey, that is, the plot. A plot with a carefully calculated shape. That plot must be presented and satisfactorily completed in each volume in the epic, not just the first or the last one. In Appendix C, I've included a checklist on "world-building," which I think may be useful for those creating adventures set in worlds other than our own. But I tweaked the worksheet so that, as you work your way down the list, you're constantly reminded to keep your plot goals in mind. How will this innovation help my character resolve his inner conflict? How will this aspect of the world intensify the personal conflict?

Some of you may have been exposed to this idea that there are only so many plots, and we unimaginative writers just keep rewriting them over and over again. E.M. Forster said there were only two plots: someone goes on a journey, or a stranger comes to town. Ronald Tobias says there are twenty master plots. Carlo Gozzi said there are thirty-six basic dramatic situations. Rudyard Kipling said there were sixty-nine plots (but I think he was kidding—he never explained what they were).

Well, they're all wrong, and frankly, I'm shocked—*shocked!*--by this rampant cynicism. Imagine attempting to reduce the complexity of storytelling to such simple templates. Here's the reality of the situation:

There are only five plots.

The Basic Plots

When I say there are only five plots, I'm not being cynical or reductionist. It's just a fact. You can go all the way back to *Gilgamesh*, and you will still only find five plots.

Whether the writer chiseled his story onto stone tablets or dictated it onto a tablet, there are still basically five plots.

But perhaps in this instance I need to understand what it is I mean by plot. I know you are capable of endlessly inventing innovative stuff to happen to your characters. Gilgamesh didn't have cell phones, and your character may not use a broadsword. But here I'm referring to the overall shape of the plot, or to what many, including Christopher Vogler, have called The Hero's Journey.

Your character is on a journey from one place to another, and all the events that occur along the way are what get him there. That's what we're discussing here. How to shape your plot to make that character journey a reality.

If you've studied the work of Carl Jung, you'll be familiar with his concept of archetypes. Jung's theory, the one that distanced him permanently from his mentor, Freud, was that humans possess a collective unconscious. Jung argued that our minds possess fundamental universal structures. These structures have external analogies that we find inherently interesting because they are hardwired into our brains. That may be why these transformations, these five plots I'm about to describe, have such universal appeal.

External action is capable of endless invention, meaning it can involve endlessly different details. But unless human beings change radically from what they have been for all of recorded history, the arc of these Jungian inner journeys can be categorized according to five basic forms.

The Education Plot

This is the most common plot and the one you are most likely writing. Others call this the maturation plot or the coming-of-age story. In the English department, we call it a bildungsroman (if it involves a male protagonist). They are all different ways of saying the same thing:

The protagonist learns something. Or grows as a person. Or comes to see life in a healthier, more positive way. One way or another, the protagonist is a better person at the end of the book than she was at the beginning—as a direct result of the trials and challenges she faced along the way.

There are so many examples of this I wonder if it's even worth singling them out. Pick your three favorite books of all time, and most of them are probably education plots, even the ones you read in childhood. The hero of *Green Eggs and Ham* learns not to be afraid to try something new. The boy hearing the story of The Lorax learns that we must take care of our planet. The Horatio Alger "rags-to-riches" novels were designed to teach young men to work hard and save their money (although there always seemed to be a heretofore unknown wealthy uncle who pulls the deserving hero out of poverty in the last chapter).

Pride and Prejudice is all about education, as the title practically screams. Before they can come together as a loving couple, Darcy must learn to be less proud (a common fault of his class at the time) and less prejudiced (against these country bumpkins he has thrown in with). Similarly, Elizabeth must be less proud about the slights Darcy has shown her family and less also prejudiced—especially when the prejudice is based upon completely unsubstantiated gossip (a problem still rife today).

In *To Kill a Mockingbird*, our viewpoint character, the little girl called Scout, learns many lessons, making it her education and coming-of-age story. Because the book was originally a collection of short stories, it is somewhat fragmented, but in each of the fragments, Scout learns a different valuable lesson. In the longest story, the trial, she learns first, that her father is the bravest man in town, and second, that even the bravest man and the best lawyer doesn't always prevail. In other fragments, she learns that the so-called monster next door may actually be a harmless pussycat. And she learns that the real monster may be the man who looks just like everyone else.

For much of Jay McInerney's *Bright Lights, Big City*, you may feel as if you're reading a party book, a male version of chick lit, about an irresponsible man skipping from one situation to the next, like the reckless hero of J.P. Donleavy's *The Ginger Man*, always moving, never settling, never committing. That impression ends when we learn the truth about this character, or specifically, what exactly he's running from. He does eventually learn to deal with it, which allows him to move forward in a more responsible manner. That's an education plot.

Did you read or see *The Devil Wore Prada*? The book is a riot, and the fact that I'm a guy didn't make Lauren Weisberger's book one whit less entertaining. Basically, our heroine wants to be a journalist but instead ends up in the fashion world. She does well for herself, but ultimately realizes that this superficial world of color-coordination and accessorizing is not for her, regardless of how profitable it might be. She returns home and writes fiction, her first love. She learns it's more important to be happy than to be rich.

Okay, so now I've given you a couple of classics, a contemporary novel, and a well regarded piece of chick lit. Are you convinced? Education stories are all over the literary world—for a reason. Readers love them, because if you have posited your reader squarely within the character's viewpoint, they will feel as if they have learned the same lessons the character did. They will feel they have grown as a person, just as the character did. They will feel they've been rewarded for the time they spent reading your book. That's the sort of reaction that makes a book stand out in a reader's mind, which is why this plot format is so popular.

The Disillusionment Plot

The disillusionment plot is sort of the sad second cousin to the education plot. As with the education plot, the protagonist changes as a result of the events of the story. Instead of changing in a positive way, however, the character changes in a deeply negative way. In other words, the protagonist experiences a profound change in worldview, but from an optimistic one to a pessimistic one.

This, as you might imagine, is more frequently employed in literary fiction than in popular fiction, but there are no rules, and as I have written elsewhere, these two largely useless distinctions are eroding more and more every day.

If *The Adventures of Huckleberry Finn* is not the greatest American novel (and it is), then *The Great Gatsby* must be. These two novels represent an amazing inversion of the persona of the writer and what they actually wrote. Twain, the notorious cynic, wrote a novel that celebrates America's triumph over our greatest mistake. F. Scott Fitzgerald, the Jazz Age party boy admired by many, wrote a novel exposing the great lie known as The American Dream.

First, recall that the viewpoint character is not the title character, Jay Gatsby (originally Gatz, a name change made to disguise ethnicity), but Nick Carraway. Nick idolizes Gatsby because in his eyes, Gatsby has it all. Tons of money (made illegally, bootlegging), stylish clothes, eternally flowing champagne, fancy cars, beautiful women fawning over him. Yes, Gatsby has everything…except the one thing he wants most. Daisy Buchanan, the girl from his past, the one who got away and is now married to another man. Even when, toward the end, Daisy is willing to run off with Gatsby, fate cruelly steps in and curtails that plan in a manner that ends with Daisy back with her husband and Gatsby bleeding to death in a swimming pool.

Turns out the American Dream wasn't all it was cracked up to be. Perhaps Fitzgerald is suggesting that evaluating success on such superficial terms is the sign of a society with seriously misplaced values. But there is no doubting that the once buoyant Nick Carraway ends the book extremely disillusioned (as do the protagonists of most of the so-called "lost generation" books).

If you've read "Heart of Darkness," Joseph Conrad's masterpiece, I don't have to explain the disillusionment. Marlowe floats up the Congo to track down Kurtz, but what he finds is how quickly men disintegrate, unrestrained by law. People can debate the meaning of Kurtz' final words, "The horror…the horror." But I think he's talking about the horror that is us. For both Marlowe and Kurtz, this is a disillusioning novel. *Lord of the Flies* strikes a similar disillusioning note about so-called civilization.

Macbeth starts out ambitious but also determined to be a better king than Duncan. He ends up so disillusioned that he soliloquizes about why anyone would even attempt to face this heartbreaking world. "Life is but a walking shadow, a poor player, that struts and frets his hour upon the stage, and then is heard no more; it is a tale told by an idiot, full of sound and fury, signifying nothing."

Hard to get more disillusioned than that.

Dickens's most disillusioning novel (and thus perhaps his most popular with academics) is *Great Expectations*. The plot is too complex to recount here, but suffice to say that Pip begins with great expectations that are not realized. His benefactor turns out to be someone very different from whom he believed it to be. And poor Pip doesn't even end up with the love interest in the end (although the door is left slightly ajar in the novel version).

I have to finish this discussion with one of the greatest novels of the twentieth century, *One Hundred Years of Solitude* by Gabriel Garcia Marquez. It's hard to explain why this magnificent work of magic realism is so extraordinary. You just need to read it. Basically it tells the story of a great family in the Columbian city of Macondo over the course of a century. The family has its highs and lows, but it ends on a note so horrific I can't even describe it in this book. And if that's not bad enough, our final protagonist, Aureliano, learns that the tragic end was foretold from the start. Despite his high aspirations, life is bad, and it's not getting any better, because "races condemned to one hundred years of solitude did not have a second opportunity on earth."

You might well wonder what the point is of writing a book that ends on such a negative note. I don't have a good answer to that question, which is why I have rarely, if ever, done it. Even if life doesn't work out perfectly for my characters in the end, I try to leave the reader with some positive takeaway, some upbeat note, something that prevents them from closing the book and wanting to stick their head in an oven. But some readers believe this kind of negativity is more realistic, and it often draws stronger reviews from literary critics than a book with a positive end.

PERFECTING PLOT

You must do what's right for the story you want to tell and the message you want to convey.

The Testing Plot

In this plot, the protagonist is tested by incredible, overwhelming opposition, but despite all odds, refuses to give up. After the education plot, this is the most popular plot.

This will be the plot of almost every action-adventure story, every thriller, every suspense novel. But you can find it in older and more classical literature as well. Homer's *The Odyssey* is the story of one man's struggle to get home to his wife, Penelope, after being away at war for twenty years (or perhaps forty, depending upon how you translate it). Odysseus is tested repeatedly, by Circe, Calypso, the sirens, Polyphemus. But each time he prevails—because he wants to get back to the faithful woman who has been stalling a suite of suitors desperate to make her their bride. *The Odyssey* is about 2800 years old—but it's still a good story, so good its plot has been completely borrowed by more recent books such as *Cold Mountain* and films such as *Brother, Where Art Thou?*

In the Bible, the *Book of Job* is a testing plot. God and Satan get together to see if they can tempt God's most faithful servant from his virtuous life. It doesn't work, but they put the man through one hellacious situation after another in what seems like a perverse spiritual chess match.

Hemingway's *The Old Man and the Sea* is a testing plot. This book, only about eighty pages in length, could not be simpler. An older man goes out in a boat to see if he's still got what it takes. He catches a blue marlin, a fish much too big for him to reel in with his equipment and his little boat, but he refuses to give up. The titanic struggle goes on for hours, the man weakens, but he refuses to cave. In the end, the boat is all but destroyed, the fish is largely ruined, the man is all but dead—but he brings the fish in. He is tested and he wins.

For contemporary readers, the Harry Potter books relate a testing plot, though one that goes on for seven volumes, with Harry tested repeatedly until he finally vanquishes Voldemort. On a more thematic level, of course, what's being tested is the power of love. Harry's mother saved him with the power of love, and it's Harry's great love for his friends that ultimately allows him to prevail.

The Hunger Games is, despite its considerable complexity, a testing plot, which has unfortunately led to a slew of imitative books involving teenagers slaughtering one another. Katniss, to save her little sister, volunteers herself for the hunger games, a brutal combat she is almost certain to lose. During a game that goes on for chapter after chapter, she's tested in about every way possible. Obviously, her physical endurance is tested. Her spirit is tested. Her friendship (of sorts) with Peeta is tested. But she prevails. In fact, she prevails so well she manages to save more than just herself, an ending I don't think any reader could predict.

Readers love testing plots. That's why so many of those ancient works are heroic fiction. We love to see strong and courageous people surmounting challenges. In real life, we might not do as well, and in truth, the opportunity will probably not arise anyway. But through the enormous power of books, we can experience that testing and triumph vicariously.

The Redemption Plot

This plot is not entirely different from the education plot, and I've heard people suggest the two should be combined, but I think there's value in considering them separately, because ultimately they tell fundamentally different stories in different ways.

In a redemption plot, the bad guy turns good, or redeems himself for past errors. So there are elements of education and maturation—but something more as well. Because the word "redemption" suggests that the protagonist has done something for which he needs to atone.

The redemption plot can be found in all levels of storytelling—in something as simple as *A Christmas Carol* (a miser is frightened into redeeming himself for a life of insensitivity and greed) to *The Dirty Dozen* (convicts are given a chance to regain their freedom by going on a suicide mission). You can even find it in Dr. Seuss. Remember, despite all the callousness that occupies most of the book—the Grinch does ultimately save Christmas.

The classic redemption story is Victor Hugo's *Les Miserables*, which you may know from the book (I hope) or the numerous film adaptations or the rapturous musical. Basically, Jean Valjean was sent to prison for stealing bread to feed his sister's starving children. He's there nineteen years. When he gets out, he can't find work or even a place to stay because he's a convict. A local bishop is kind enough to feed him and let him spend the night at the vicarage.

Valjean rewards the man's kindness by stealing the his plates and silverware and fleeing.

91

When the gendarmes haul him back to the bishop, Valjean knows full well that as soon as the bishop acknowledges that he was robbed, Valjean will be convicted and sent to prison for the rest of his life. But the bishop doesn't do that. Instead he says (I'm paraphrasing), "Jean, why'd you leave so soon? I wanted you to take the silver candlesticks, too."

So the gendarmes leave, and Valjean, the thief, is saved. The bishop looks him in the eye and says, "Now your life belongs to God."

Valjean lives his life exactly that way, first establishing a new identity, then building a prosperous factory, employing those in need, aiding the tragic Fantine, and ultimately raising little Cosette as if she were his own daughter, even risking his life to save the man Cosette loves. Why does he go to such extreme measures?

To redeem himself for his past mistakes. To make himself a better man than he was before.

Joseph Conrad's *Lord Jim* is a brilliant redemption novel. The problem is that it's so challenging to read, given its non-chronological storytelling and its multiple levels of diegesis. (*Lord Jim* may represent the only time I've advised people to watch the film first so they can better follow the book). Lord Jim is a British naval officer. The *Patna* starts taking on water and they think it's going down, so they decide to abandon ship. Two problems: 1) they leave the passengers behind, and 2) officers are supposed to go down with their ships.

They make it safely to shore, but they soon hear devastating news. The *Patna* didn't sink. The passengers made it safely to shore. So they not only abandoned ship— they're branded as cowards. Jim is drummed out of the navy.

Many years later, Jim is helping and ultimately leading natives on the tiny island of Patusan somewhere in the South Seas. After a struggle with a marauder known as "Gentlemen" Brown, Jim gives his life to save the people. They have no idea why this man they call "Lord" is helping them. But we do. Because we know the backstory. We know Jim is attempting to redeem himself for the sins of his past.

Let me give you one last example: Dickens's *A Tale of Two Cities*. If you haven't read this one, I hope you will. It's just as thrilling and inspiring today as it was a hundred and fifty years ago. The protagonist is Sydney Carton, a failed, washed-up dissipated barrister. Nice enough fellow, but a flop in life. He has a great love, Lucie, and she's kind to him, but she's never going to commit to such a mess. She marries Charles Darnay—a man who looks very much like Sydney. Darnay is caught up in the middle of the French Revolution, locked up in the Bastille, and sentenced to die.

But a surprising event occurs. While the husband sits in his cold cell awaiting his doom, Sydney Carton breaks in. Sydney knows they can't both escape but thinks they might be able to bring off a substitution, especially given the strong physical resemblance. So he drugs Darnay and takes the man's place. Darnay escapes and Sydney goes to the guillotine in his stead.

Now, some guys might have thought, Hey, with the husband out of the way, maybe my chances with Lucie will improve. But Sydney didn't. His love for her was so great that he was willing to die to save the man he knew deserved the affection of the woman he loved. There could be no stronger love than that. And nothing greater than the redemptive power of love. Sydney salvages a wasted life with a triumphal act of redemption. He approaches the blade bravely stating (the famous words that would be used by Spock three hundred years later), "It is a far, far better thing that I do, than I have ever done; it is a far, far better rest that I go to than I have ever known."

The appeal of the redemption plot is easy to explain. I can do it in one sentence: We've all screwed up. And when those unfortunate errors occur, we'd like to think we could somehow do something to compensate for them. These fictional characters I've mentioned did. And reading about them gives readers the hope that they might be able to find salvation as well.

The Corruption Plot

The fifth and last of the five plots is in some respects related to the disillusionment plot, but it's not the same. It's possible to be disillusioned without being corrupted, and it's possible to be corrupted without being disillusioned. So it's useful to consider the two separately, understanding that neither is likely to lead to the stories that leave readers with that "Up with People" feeling in their hearts.

In the redemption plot, the bad guy turns good. In the corruption plot, the good guy turns bad.

It happens. Even in real life. People can be so easily tempted by so much. Money. Envy. Lust. Substance abuse. Sloth. Gossip. Backstabbing. The list is endless.

To me the classic corruption plot is *The Treasure of the Sierra Madre*, which I hope you know either from B. Traven's excellent book or from John Huston's excellent film adaptation. To pair it down to the essence: three guys go prospecting for gold. Our lead character, Fred C.

Dobbs, isn't evil. He starts out as someone you'd like to have breakfast with, not Voldemort. But the gold changes him, or rather, the pursuit of gold, the lust for gold, the fear that he might be cheated.

People often misquote the Bible. It's not money that's the root of all evil. It's the *love* of money that's the root of all evil. And that's what happens to Dobbs, ultimately leading to a tragic end.

Let's consider a more positive protagonist. How about sweet Tess from the Hardy book I mentioned earlier, *Tess of the d'Urbervilles*. She comes from a poor family, but they believe they're related to wealthier folks not far away, so they send Tess to see if the rich relations can do anything for her. Turns out, they aren't related at all—the wealthy family bought the title. But the libertine Alec does take in Tess, showing her a life of comfort and ease and beauty she has never seen before. He can promise her a better life…with certain conditions. It takes a while, but Tess is corrupted. In the end, in an act of desperate despair, she murders her corrupter.

Faust, depending upon which version you're reading, is tempted by the lust for power, or knowledge, or Helen of Troy. But selling your soul to the devil is a fairly bad case of corruption. Othello is corrupted by Iago's gossiping and manipulating and ends up killing Desdemona, the newlywed bride he loves so dearly. Willie Stark in Robert Penn Warren's *All the King's Men* starts off as an idealistic lawyer who wants to help the people, but politics corrupts him.

Corruption stories are cautionary tales. People read them not because they enjoy seeing nice people ruined but because it reminds them to resist whatever temptations led those characters astray.

Are you forced to write only one of these plots? No. It is entirely possible that your story has elements of more than one. But one should dominate. You may have an education plot with some testing elements in it, no problem. But if the plot has too many, it will become a mishmash going in too many directions at once, and the reader will be confused and dissatisfied at the end. Commit to primarily telling one of these plots. And then tell it in the best possible way you can.

Why Do I Need to Know This?

You may be wondering what the point is of reducing every story ever told to five plots. Am I trying to make your writing formulaic or cliché? Absolutely not. But I want you to understand the way stories work so that you can tell a better one. Don't resist these plots—embrace them. Figure out which one you're telling, then start rearranging the scenes in your outline so you can tell it in the most effective way possible. Use these plots to your advantage. They will enrich your writing.

If your protagonist isn't on one of these journeys, then you're probably not writing a novel. An episode, maybe, a slice-of-life, a series of interesting incidents. But not a novel. These journeys are more than just good ideas.

They define story.

Study these plots and decide which one you want to tell. So much of plotting has to do with finding the right match. What character is best for my plot? What plot is best for my character? What subplots best fit my primary conflict? What inner, personal, and external conflicts best work together? And which plot structure will bring it all together in a brilliant union of storytelling and talent?

PERFECTING PLOT

Don't be discouraged if you can't get it right in the first draft. Just keep writing. And rewriting. And if you refuse to quit, the day will come when you do get it all right. And that's when you get published.

Highlights

1) There are only five plots.

2) In the Education Plot, the protagonist learns something, or grows as a person, or comes to see life in a healthier, more positive way.

3) In the Disillusionment Plot, the protagonist experiences a profound change in worldview, but from a positive one to a negative one.

4) In the Testing Plot, the antagonist is challenged by incredible, overwhelming opposition, but despite all odds refuses to give up.

5) In the Redemption Plot, the protagonists redeem themselves for sins, errors, or crimes of the past.

6) In the Corruption Plot, an initially good person is negatively altered by something that occurs during the story.

7) The purpose of understanding which plot you're writing is not to make your work formulaic or cliché, but rather to enhance it. If you know what story you're telling, you're likely to do a better job of telling it.

PERFECTING PLOT

Red Sneaker Exercises

Which plot are you writing? You need to know. Here are some questions that might help you arrive at an answer:

1) What does your protagonist want or desire more than anything else in the world?

2) A character arc is typically a journey from one place to its dialectical opposite. What's your main character's arc? How are you going to show the character's change over the course of the book?

3) You've tried to match your main character to your plot and your plot to your character in a symbiotic relationship that enhances both. Why do they work well together?

4) What kind of opposition will your protagonist face? What does that opposition represent?

5) What metaphor does your lead character represent?

6) What are you trying to say with this book?

7) What emotion do you want readers to feel as they turn the last page of your book?

8) If you had one minute during which you could simultaneously broadcast a message to all people in all

languages—what would you say? Does your story convey the same message?

APPENDIX A: Inner Conflicts

Here's a list of the internal factors that commonly create inner conflict. Which one might be right for your protagonist?

Insecurity

Regret or remorse

Guilt

Passion

Lust

Weakness

Obligation

Hope

Honor

Pride

Nobility

Integrity

Desperation

Fear

WILLIAM BERNHARDT

Addiction

Childhood trauma

Psychological illness

APPENDIX B: PERSONAL CONFLICTS

According to a major study, these are the events that are the most traumatizing, meaning they have the greatest potential for radically disrupting a person's life. I've listed them in descending order from the worst to the least (which is still pretty bad). Would any of them enrich your story by creating more personal conflict?

Don't use them all. That would just be too much to bear.

Death of a spouse

Divorce/Separation

Imprisonment

Death of a close family member

Personal injury or illness

Marriage

Dismissal from Work

WILLIAM BERNHARDT

Retirement

Health change

Pregnancy

Sexual difficulties

APPENDIX C: WORLD-BUILDING

How is your world different from Earth? Why? Were these changes made arbitrarily, or do they relate directly to the main character, the plot, or the theme? Will these changes enhance the marriage of character and plot, or complicate the three levels of conflict, or emphasize the plot you're telling?

(You might find it useful to go through this list even if you're not writing a science fiction or fantasy novel.)

What does your world look like?

What's the local history?

What do the people look like?

Do they have traditional rituals that differ from ours? If so, what are they and how did they develop?

Is this world technologically different from ours? Do these differences relate to the character or what you're trying to say with the book? Or are they just random futurism (i.e. flying cars)?

Is this a world of magic or a world of science?

What's the geography of this world? Have you drawn a map? Geography often influences how people live and what they believe.

How does the political system work?

What is the predominant religion? Often, politics and religion can be the most profound influences on how people think and consequently how they act.

How do the people live? What does your protagonist do in his or her spare time? Do they have special skills that become useful later or explain why they are embarking on this particular quest? Do they have hobbies that tell us something about the world you've created?

What kind of medicine exists?

Are there laws? How are they enforced?

Is it a capitalistic society? Is there some sort of barter, trade, or currency?

How much do you know about the arts, entertainment, fashion, youth fads, or slang of your world?

APPENDIX D: SYNOPSIS

The most difficult part of writing a synopsis is trying to get the essential details of your story down to a page or so without making it completely boring. Don't be discouraged if you don't get it right the first time. Or the tenth. Writing a good synopsis can be extremely challenging.

Agents (and editors) differ in their requirements, but generally they will ask for a synopsis in one or two pages, single-spaced. These people are busy, so if you can do it well in one page, you should.

Generally speaking, a good synopsis will be composed of three sections:

1) The first section identifies your protagonist, primary conflict, and setting. Agents are always looking for something different, particularly a fresh point of view. Focus on how can you make your story *not* sound like every other book of this type.

2) The next section should convey any major plot turns or conflicts and any characters that should be mentioned so your book summary will make sense to whoever reads it. Basically, it should describe the narrative arc of the book. Make sure you explain the protagonist's actions and motivations in a way that makes sense and doesn't sound cliché. But don't get so swept up in telling all the details of the story that you forget to describe the emotions your characters experience. Human emotion is what makes a story powerful.

3) In the final section, indicate how the major conflicts are resolved. Yes, you give away the ending and any major surprises. The synopsis should be a clear presentation of your novel that doesn't leave the reader confused. You aren't likely to sell your book by leaving out the best parts.

Please remember: agents are looking for people who can write well. If your synopsis doesn't shine, why would anyone look at your manuscript? Focus on clarity, precision, and concision. You don't have enough space to waste words.

Here are the primary mistakes aspiring writers make when writing synopses:

1) Don't try to cram in too many characters and plot details. You can't get it all in. Focus on what is necessary to understand the narrative arc. Eliminate unnecessary details, descriptions, and backstory.

2) Avoid "writerly" writing. Just tell the story. In other words, no genre jargon, no references to other books, no creative-writing-class terms of art. Don't say, "In a flashback, Aura sees that…" Don't say, "This is a coming-of-age story in which…"

3) Don't try to inject emotion or excitement into your synopsis with adverbs or clichés. I understand it's difficult to convey the emotional content of your story in so few words. Do the best you can. But don't resort to saying, "In a poignant scene, Aura…" or "In a hilarious

moment of mistaken identity…" Your story must speak for itself, even in the synopsis.

4) Don't make the mistake of writing back cover copy instead of a synopsis. This is not the time to use generalizations or to withhold important details to increase the agent's interest. A good opening tagline might be an effective teaser, but don't write the whole synopsis that way.

WILLIAM BERNHARDT

APPENDIX E: The Writer's Calendar

Is it possible to finish a top-quality manuscript in six months? Yes, if you're willing to do the work necessary to make it happen. Here's a plan.

Week 1

Commit to your writing schedule.

Find your writing place.

Sign the Writer's Contract in Appendix F. Inform friends and family.

Think about what you want to write. Start thinking like a writer.

Week 2

Commit to a premise—then make it bigger. Is it big and unique enough to attract a publisher's attention?

Commit to a genre. What's your spin on the genre? How will you make it the same—but different? Research as needed.

Week 3

Develop your main protagonist and antagonist.

Complete Character Detail Sheets (found in *Creating Character*) for both. What are their best qualities—and worst? What drives them?

What is your protagonist's character arc? What does he/she want, seek, desire? How will your character change over the course of the book?

Write a half-page example of dialogue for each major character in their distinct voice.

Week 4

Put all major events (scenes) on index cards, approximately sixty total (as described in the book on structure).

Arrange the cards by Acts. Highlight the Plot Turning Points and Character Turning Points.

Type the index cards into an outline, adding detail when you have it.

Week 5

Think about the shape of your story—the Plot. Will your character experience growth? Maturity? Redemption? Disillusionment?

Map out well-planned and planted surprises to maintain reader interest. What is the last occurrence the reader will suspect?

Don't shy away from a great scene because it doesn't fit your story as you currently understand it. See if you can change the story to accommodate the great scene.

Weeks 6-18

Write at least five pages every day—ten on Saturdays. No editing. Just keep moving ahead.

Do additional writing as necessary to complete 10% each week.

Week 19-21

Perform triage on what you've written. Revise. Then revise more. Reference the Revision lecture on the *Fundamentals of Fiction* DVD to spot potential problems.

Week 22-24

Give the manuscript to trusted beta readers.

Reread it yourself, focusing on character consistency, character depth. Are the characters sympathetic or empathetic?

Reread it focusing on plot, pacing, story logic, theme. Is the story plausible? Obtain comments from readers. Incorporate comments from readers where appropriate.

Reread it focusing on dialogue.

Set it aside for a time, then reread it with fresh eyes. Do you see problems you didn't spot before?

And then—

Attend writing conferences and bounce your ideas off agents and editors. If people don't ask to see your manuscript, your premise needs work. If people ask to see pages but don't take you on, your manuscript is not ready. Consider attending a small-group writing seminar to give your book the final editing or stylistic work it needs to be publishable.

WILLIAM BERNHARDT

APPENDIX F: The Writer's Contract

I, _____, hereinafter known as "the Writer," in consideration of these premises, hereby agree as follows:

1) The aforementioned Writer agrees that he/she will undertake a long-term, intensive writing project. The Writer agrees to work ___ hours a day, regardless of external distractions or personal circumstances. The Writer agrees to maintain this schedule until the writing project is completed.

2) The Writer understands that this is a difficult task and that there will be days when he/she does not feel like writing or when others will attempt to make demands upon the Writer's time. The Writer will not allow this to interfere with the completion of the agreement made in paragraph one (1) of this contract.

3) The Writer understands that good physical and mental health is essential to the completion of any writing project. Therefore, in order to complete the agreement made in paragraph one (1), the Writer commits to a serious program of self-care, which shall include but shall not be limited to: adequate sleep, healthy diet, exercise, the relinquishment of bad habits, and reading time.

_____

Signature of The Writer and Witnesses

_____

Date Signed

WILLIAM BERNHARDT

APPENDIX G: The Writer's Reading List

The Chicago Manual of Style. 16th ed. Chicago: University of Chicago Press, 2010.

Cook, Vivian. *All in a Word: 100 Delightful Excursions into the Uses and Abuses of Words.* Brooklyn: Melville House, 2010.

Fowler, H.W. *Fowler's Modern English Usage.* 3rd ed. Rev. Ernest Gowers. N.Y. & Oxford: Oxford University Press, 2004.

Goldman, William. *Adventures in the Screen Trade: A Personal View of Hollywood and Screenwriting.* New York: Grand Central, 1989.

Hale, Constance. *Sin and Syntax: How to Create Wickedly Effective Prose.* New York: Broadway Books, 2001.

Hart, Jack. *A Writer's Coach: The Complete Guide to Writing Strategies That Work.* New York: Anchor Books, 2006.

Jones, Catherine Ann. *The Way of Story: The Craft and Soul of Writing.* Studio City: Michael Wiese Productions, 2007.

Klauser, Henriette Anne. *Writing on Both Sides of the Brain.* San Francisco: Harper & Row, 1987.

Maass, Donald. *The Fire in Fiction: Passion, Purpose, and Techniques to Make Your Novel Great.* Cincinnati: Writers Digest Books, 2009.

Maass, Donald. *Writing the Breakout Novel: Insider Advice for Taking Your Fiction to the Next Level.* Cincinnati: Writers Digest Books, 2001.

Maass, Donald. *Writing 21st Century Fiction: High Impact Techniques for Exceptional Storytelling.* Cincinnati: Writers Digest Books, 2012.

O'Conner, Patricia T. *Woe Is I: The Grammarphobe's Guide to Better English in Plain English.* 2nd ed. New York: Riverhead Books, 2003.

O'Conner, Patricia T. *Origins of the Specious: Myths and Misconceptions of the English Language.* New York: Random House, 2009.

Strunk, William, Jr., and White, E.B. *The Elements of Style.* 4th ed. N.Y.: Macmillan, 2000.

Truss, Lynne. *Eats Shoots & Leaves: The Zero Tolerance Guide to Punctuation.* New York: Gotham Books, 2005.

Vogler, Christopher. *The Writer's Journey: Mythic Structure for Storytellers and Screenwriters.* Studio City: Michael Wiese Productions, 1992.

Zinsler, William. *On Writing Well: The Classic Guide to Writing Nonfiction.* 30th Anniv. Ed.   New York: Harper Perennial, 2006.

WILLIAM BERNHARDT

About the Author

William Bernhardt is the bestselling author of more than thirty books, including the blockbuster Ben Kincaid series of novels. In addition, Bernhardt founded the Red Sneaker Writing Center in 2005, hosting writing workshops and small-group seminars and becoming one of the most in-demand writing instructors in the nation. His programs have educated many authors now published at major New York houses. He holds a Masters Degree in English Literature and is the only writer to have received the Southern Writers Guild's Gold Medal Award, the Royden B. Davis Distinguished Author Award (University of Pennsylvania) and the H. Louise Cobb Distinguished Author Award (Oklahoma State), which is given "in recognition of an outstanding body of work that has profoundly influenced the way in which we understand ourselves and American society at large." In addition to the novels, he has written plays, including a musical (book and music), humor, nonfiction books, children books, biography, poetry, and crossword puzzles. He is a member of the Author's Guild, PEN International and the American Academy of Poets.

Made in the USA
Lexington, KY
12 September 2013